THE CHIEF REINVENTION OFFICER HANDBOOK

HOW TO THRIVE IN CHAOS

THE CHIEF REINVENTION OFFICER HANDBOOK

How to Thrive in Chaos

WRITTEN BY
Nadya Zhexembayeva

CO-CREATED BY
A community of 3,000+ reinventors
from 40+ countries

DESIGNED BY
Maxim Gorbach & Ilya Galushin, PRESIUM

IDEAPRESS
PUBLISHING

Printed in Canada.

IDEAPRESS PUBLISHING | WWW.IDEAPRESSPUBLISHING.com

All trademarks are the property of their respective companies.

COVER AND BOOK DESIGN by PRESIUM

First Printing: October 2020
Cataloging-in-Publication Data is on file with the Library of Congress.

ISBN: 978-1-646870-32-5

SPECIAL SALES

Ideapress Books are available at a special discount for bulk purchases for sales promotions and premiums, educational institutions or for use in corporate training programs. Special editions, including personalized covers, custom forewords and bonus content are also available. For more information, email info@ideapresspublishing.com

To the Chief Reinvention Officer within you.

Titanic Syndrome

| tī-ˈta-nik ˈsin-drōm|, noun

A corporate disease in which organizations facing disruption create their own downfall through **arrogance, excessive attachment to past success,** or **inability to recognize and adapt to the new and emerging reality.**

Reinvention

|rēinˈven(t)SHən|, noun

1. A practice of **embracing** change by **reimagining and remaking** something so that it manifests new and **improved** attributes, qualities, and results.

2. A **systematic** approach to thriving in chaos that includes ongoing anticipation, design, and implementation of change **via continuous sense-making, anticipatory and emergent learning,** and **synthesis** of cross-boundary, cross-disciplinary, and cross-functional knowledge.

3. A way to foster **sustainability** of a system by **dynamically harmonizing** continuity and change.

4. An **immune system** designed to ensure systematic health for individuals and organizations.

5. A **structured** and **deliberate** effort to engage in **healthy cycles of planned renewal,** building on the past to ensure current and future viability.

AN INTRODUCTION

CHANGE

IS NOT A PROJECT

CHANGE IS NOT A PROJECT

On January 11, 2020, Chinese media reported the first novel coronavirus death, a sixty-one-year-old man. In the months that followed, the world suffered millions of infections and mourned hundreds of thousands of deaths from what became known as COVID-19.

Suffering struck many organizations, communities, and livelihoods as well. In the United States alone, 30 million people filed for unemployment by May 2020. Century-old companies, passed down for generations, disappeared seemingly overnight. Entire careers vanished.

Yet, as in every global upheaval before, the suffering went hand in hand with courage. Medical professionals worked unimaginable miracles to save the infected. Grocery workers packed food for all to eat. Bus drivers continued to connect the communities. Businesses took on the chaos and fought to make lives a little bit easier — or a lot.

Before COVID-19 put much of the world on lockdown, Miro was a nine-year-old company with 280 employees and a respectable following of 3.5 million users. Designed to deliver a collaborative virtual experience for a team of people working on a digital whiteboard, Miro's flexible solution mimics the experience of sitting together for a brainstorming session even if team members are dispersed around the world, sitting on their own couches in sweats.

Like many other virtual collaboration providers, Miro recognized and embraced the growing trend of teams needing to work together while separated in space and time. Most solution providers, however, made their bets on offering a simple but relatively rigid structure, still requiring more sophisticated and unstructured collaborations to be done in person. Miro went a different way, offering extreme freedom and flexibility of use, allowing for infinite ways to use the virtual board (digital "sticky" notes included).

Andrey Khusid, Miro's CEO, explains: "My interest in the power of visual communication and collaboration began more than a decade ago when I was running a design agency. From the start, our product gained traction among people who usually relied on physical whiteboards but had to collaborate with people in different locations: designers, product managers, scrum masters, agile coaches, project managers, program managers, strategists. We got immediate feedback that our product was solving a real problem for so many remote workers and distributed teams."

As the virus forced people to stay indoors and away from their offices, Miro grew its base to five million users and 21,000 paying customers, including such household names as Dell, Salesforce, PwC, Electronic Arts, Verizon, and Deloitte. Educators and non-profit leaders joined in as well. Because of Miro, critical solutions were developed, deep insights were secured, jobs were saved, learning opportunities were pro-

tected, and projects got lifted off the ground, shutdown be damned.

Miro saw a significant change in quality, not just quantity of customer experience: Larger collaborative sessions with twenty to twenty-nine simultaneous participants on a board in a given week soared 1,807% in mid-April compared with early March. Meanwhile, the total time spent

video chatting increased by a whopping 2,379% in April compared with March. The world was clearly ready to re-invent virtual collaboration.

As many companies got crushed by the waves of pandemic destruction and sank to the bottom of the economic ocean, Miro managed to pull some survivors out of the murky waters and offer them jobs.

By April 23, 2020, the company landed a hefty $50 million Series B investment, had more than 330 employees, and announced plans to hire 150 more by the end of the year.

Miro's story of thriving and serving in crisis is neither an exception nor an accident.

In 2010, in the middle of another crisis, researchers Ranjay Gulati, Nitin Nohria, and Franz Wohlgezogen showed that during the recessions of 1980, 1990, and 2000, 17% of the 4,700 public companies they studied did not survive. They went bankrupt, were acquired, or simply were dismantled. Such fates are expected in any significant wave of change, but here is what was striking. Nine percent of the companies not only survived the chaos, but also thrived, beating the competition by at least 10% in both sales and profits growth.

In 2019, Walter Frick shared a powerful Harvard Business Review article, "How to Survive a Recession and Thrive Afterward," with similar results for more recent studies done by Bain and McKinsey. During the Great Recession of 2008-2011, "the top 10% of companies in Bain's analysis saw their earnings climb steadily throughout the period and continue to rise afterward."

The goal of this book is to make sure that you avoid the fate of the bottom 17% and claim your spot in the flourishing 10%.

In the past thirty years, I have seen, lived through, and studied a wide variety of disruptions around the world. Just as with COVID-19, every time a crisis started to descend upon the globe, it unleashed a wide variety of questions. They ranged from the purely practical, such as "How do we cut costs?"; to the more managerial, such as "How do I coach my team through paralysis?"; all the way to the existential "What does it all mean for the way we live, work, and interact in the future?"

But as time goes on in every crisis, one question seems to take over most business meetings, conversations, and articles. "How do we make it until this is over?" starts an executive meeting. "How do we survive until things stabilize?" echoes a chat room for small business owners. "How do we start getting back to normal?" reiterates a business news article.

Hidden in these statements is a particular assumption: Surviving disruption is to be seen as a project — an isolated one-time event, with a clear beginning and an expected end. All we need to do to survive this crisis is to treat it like any other project, and we'll cross the finish line soon. Right?

The prevalence of this assumption in business today is not surprising.

For most of human history, we've lived in volatile and unpredictable environments. Natural disasters as well as man-made events created a world in which people, organizations, and entire countries could disappear overnight. From the Roman panic of 33 AD to the Dutch Tulip Mania of 1637, financial crises were omnipresent.

Whether your village was disrupted by plague, bankruptcy, or war, one thing was certain: Nothing was here to stay.

> **" The goal of this book is to make sure that you avoid the fate of the bottom 17% and claim your spot in the flourishing 10%.**

Yet this world of constant crisis seemed to dissolve in the second part of the twentieth century. While isolated wars and disruptions continued, all in all, things seemed to stabilize after the Second World War: no significant global conflict, relatively stable borders, no fundamental economic disruptions. It looked as if we had reached what author Francis Fukuyama memorably called "The End of History."

And that's when modern management was born. Although its foundations were laid earlier with the first collegiate school of business created in 1881, what we call management really took shape in the three decades following World War II. The classic management functions – strategy, human resource management, operations research, innovation, IT management, and more – were all professionalized in the postwar era of relative stability. Many of

our most beloved management tools and frameworks – Just-in-Time Production, Total Quality Management, and Michael Porter's Five Forces – were developed for a business environment that was relatively predictable.

For many years, the data seemed to justify the assumption of stability built into our business operating systems. As Steve Denning of Forbes puts it: "Fifty years ago, 'milking the cash cow' could go on for many decades. Half a century ago, the life expectancy of a firm in the Fortune 500 was around seventy-five years." Geoff Colvin of Fortune gives a similar number for an average life span of an S&P 500 company: sixty-one years in 1958. Corporations worldwide enjoyed long and healthy lives, with a slow rise to the top of financial performance and a gradual decline to annihilation. The rate of change was so slow, and crises were so rare that reinvention was rarely needed. When it was, we had all the time in the world to renew our business on our terms, a once-in-a-lifetime project.

However, the stable, predictable postwar world, if it ever existed, is long gone.

Although popular economic folklore highlights the Great Depression that started in 1929 and the Great Recession that erupted in 2008, there were many others. Even if we forget regional or industry-specific crises and focus only on country recessions, the number is shocking. IMD-Lausanne's Professor Emeritus Jim Ellert shows that even in the recent past, since 1988, the world has experienced 469 country recessions, which would average about one local recession every 25 days.

Beyond economic disruptions, as COVID-19 has demonstrated, our modern deeply interdependent world is experiencing turmoil in every shape and form. The World Economic Forum's 2019 Global Risk Report has mapped out thirty critical risks across five categories – economic, environmental, geopolitical, societal, and technological – and showed the connections among them. The spread of infectious disease was on that list, even making it to the top 10. COVID-19 was fully anticipated, and so were many other disruptions. To borrow from author William Gibson, "The next crisis is already here – it's just unevenly distributed."

As globalization, technology, interconnectedness, and many other trends continue to bring volatility and uncertainty to our world, we seem to be stuck with management tools and assumptions that are outdated and life-threatening to our business.

This is showing up in the longevity of today's top firms. To go back to Denning: "What's different today is that globalization and the shift in power in the marketplace from buyer to seller is dramatically shortening the life expectancy of firms that are merely milking their cash cows … Now [the life expectancy of a firm is] less than fifteen years and declining even further." That number is supported by the 2018 Corporate Longevity Forecast conducted by Innosight that showed in 1964, the S&P 500 companies would stay on the list for an average of thirty-three years. It "narrowed to twenty-four years by 2016 and is forecast to shrink to just twelve years by 2027."

> **Since 1988, the world has experienced 469 country recessions, which would average about one local recession every 25 days.**

Staying on top of the game is becoming an impossible task as well. "Only 44% of today's industry leaders have held their position for at least five years, down from 77% a half-century ago. One out of three public companies will cease to exist in their current form over the next five years – a rate six times higher than forty years ago," according to BCG, a global consulting firm.

And that brings us back to where we started: When are we going back to business as usual, where things are stable, and disruptions are rare and isolated? A world where we can manage a crisis as we would a project?

The simple answer is: Never.

Volatility is here to stay. In a world of constant flux, change cannot be treated as an isolated project. If you live in a warm climate where snow falls once in fifty years, you can look at a snowstorm as a rare isolated event to plow through. But if it snows routinely and repeatedly, you need to build a system, allocate resources, and deal with snow as if you mean it (perhaps making a bit of money on a new skiing resort and turning snow into your competitive advantage).

And that brings us back to the story of Miro. When we look at disruption as a rare event, it's easy to see the success of the company as pure luck – a story of a business being perfectly but accidentally positioned to thrive amid an unpredictable pandemic. But the success of Miro was not an accident – just as the pandemic was not unpredictable.

The company was built to capture and monetize the new and emergent reality of remote work. This trend has been explored and researched for years, but countless organizations and entire industries (think tradition-al education, event management, or office software businesses) all ignored the coming disruption.

In contrast, throughout nearly a decade of its existence, Miro turned reinvention into an art form – anticipating, designing, and implementing change again and again across products, processes, market positioning, and beyond. Want to use a virtual board but don't know where to start? Here is a template. Have your own template that works? Share it via Miroverse – the global Miro community. Need a timer to make virtual sessions easier to facilitate? Yes, it's ready. The list of reinventions is long and colorful.

In 2019, to capture its journey of deliberate consistent change, the company rebranded. Taking a considerable risk, it abandoned an established but narrowly focused brand, RealtimeBoard, to bring renewal and energy with a more universal Miro. Like many other reinventions before, this one seemed to pay off – preparing the business for the turmoil of 2020. Perhaps the old saying has been right all along: Luck is what happens when preparation meets opportunity.

And that's what this book is all about. The challenge we face isn't about trying to survive until things stabilize, but rather about learning to thrive in constant chaos. That happens only when we accept that change is no longer a project and build a well-thought-out reinvention system that works.

My goal is to help you build such a system.

> **One out of three public companies will cease to exist in their current form over the next five years – a rate six times higher than forty years ago.**

YOU ARE READING THE CHIEF REINVENTION OFFICER HANDBOOK.

BUT WHAT IS A "CHIEF REINVENTION OFFICER"?

What is "Chief Reinvention Officer"? A mindset? A method? A movement? An actual managerial position?

The answer is: All of the above.

"Chief Reinvention Officer" is a term I first coined in 2014 when Mark Levy, a brilliant management thinker and author of *Accidental Genius,* asked me: "If what you do in companies, all those decades of working with disruption and change, had a job title, what would it be?"

That was a tough question, so I went through a list of possible answers one by one. Chief Innovation Officer? No, my job is also about protecting the old. Chief Transformation Officer? We are so tired of the word *transformation,* and it so rarely produces results! Chief Strategy Officer? But what about implementation?

And then it just came out. "Chief Reinvention Officer." Mark stopped for a second (he is a tough critic, so I was bracing for impact). Then he said, "I think you should purchase the URL today."

And that was it.

By January 2015, our first reinvention manifesto was published.

By April 2015, I was speaking on the TEDx stage about why companies need Chief Reinvention Officers and why countries must establish Ministries of Reinvention.

By summertime, our lawyers were asking us to trademark. My answer was as non-negotiable as it was swift. No. We are NOT going to trademark this. Chief Reinvention Officer is a title meant to be used by as many people as possible. Even more important, Chief Reinvention Officer is a title you give yourself long before it gets instituted at your company. So absolutely not!

Imagine my surprise when that simple vision started to come to life?!

First, I changed my own title to Chief Reinvention Officer. Since most of all, Chief Reinvention Officer is a way to see the world, we gathered a global community under this banner to share reinvention resources, build new tools, and rethink the way this world works.

In the years that followed, business models, products, processes, and organizational cultures were reinvented. Lives were completely reimagined. Nonprofit organizations rebuilt themselves. All this happened while exchanging successes, accepting failures, and sharpening the tools and ideas within our reinvention tribe.

Then the movement grew, as pioneers from many corners of the world started to claim this title. The first Chief Reinvention Officer at a European manufacturing company. At a South African consultancy. Appointed to a newly created position

for the U.S. state of North Dakota. What in the world did we just start? A revolution.

Now it's your turn to join us. Without anybody's invitation. Without asking for permission. Become the Chief Reinvention Officer of your own life and perhaps of your company as well.

In a world where you are expected to change at least five careers and countless jobs per life, the one thing that will stay constant is reinvention.

So make it yours. Turn change and disruption into an opportunity. Grow reinvention into

your superpower, your core competence, your compass throughout the uncertainty, volatility, and chaos of our world.

Welcome to our global reinvention movement. We've been waiting for you.

Ready to sail?
Let's do it!

Forget programming —
the best skill to teach children
is reinvention.

Yuval Noah Harari

THE MAP

WELCOME

TO A BUSINESS BOOK, REINVENTED

THIS IS NOT YOUR USUAL BOOK

Here's the deal: Traditionally, publishing a book takes **two to three years.** From developing the content to getting the contract to going through production, this process takes a lot of time. In other words, today's "hot off the press" business books were probably **started at least two years ago — and were based on concepts and data developed half a decade earlier.**

That all seems so twentieth century!

To put it bluntly, today's speed of change doesn't allow for such a relaxed pace.

In a world where companies need to reinvent themselves every two to three years just to survive, a book based on data and ideas that are five years old simply won't do. Since this is a book about speed of change, it would be laughable to go the traditional route.

We want you to see the benchmarks and insights from our annual Global Reinvention Survey as soon as we get them — not years later.

We want you to use our diagnostic tool the moment it's tested and has proved its usefulness — not when it's too late for you to diagnose and prevent a calamity.

We want you to see the different ways that companies deal with change as it happens — not when the economic conditions make their lessons irrelevant.

We want to deliver this book into your hands just in time — and make sure you have both theoretical knowledge and pragmatic tools to deliver tangible results.

It could spell the difference between your success or failure.

That's why we're reinventing what a modern book looks like.

This is a living book.

Reinvention is not a spectator sport. Just as you cannot grow your physical muscles by reading a book about push-ups, you cannot grow your reinvention muscles by reading the words on these pages.

You have to live it.

To make sure it's as fun as it is impactful, we've made a few choices to add life to the book:

1. This is a handbook, meant to be always handy, available for a different kind of reinvention challenge. It is rich with tools and designed to be read in different ways: sequentially, from beginning to end, or non-linearly, starting with any topic or tool you find most needed right now.

2. This is a workbook, imagined to be worn out, written on top of, with at least one tool, our Business Model Reinvention Cards, to be cut out of the book and used immediately. Don't skip the practice. Do the work.

3. This is a community project. Every concept, definition, framework, and tool in this book was developed together with practicing business leaders, putting every idea and tool to the test. We've updated and reworked every worksheet, and we will continue to evolve these reinvention strategies as your business and life evolve.

HERE IS HOW IT WORKS:

You buy it once but continue to get new bonus insights and resources, including video tutorials for key concepts and tools.

To access the bonus section, make sure to sign up at **www.ChiefReinventionOfficer/resources**

Throughout the book, additional resources are featured:

- **Our own tools, such as tests, cases, and visuals,** can be used openly in your business and personal life. No permission is necessary, but if you find them useful, we do ask you to provide a reference to our work – so that we can connect and support everyone who needs reinvention most.

- **Recommended books and articles** are offered in each section as additional resources can be easily accessed. Each recommendation is carefully selected and tested for real-world impact. And if you are having trouble finding the mentioned materials, you can always go to the resource section of our website to find the links for all the recommendations and much more.

- **Our private online community,** called Reinvention Society, supports you daily as you put the new reinvention ideas and tools into practice. Here you can ask for feedback on your new product or process, see the latest cases and examples, and get your questions answered at our regular free, live Q&A sessions. You can find more information about the community in the bonus section.

" Reinvention is not a spectator sport.

A global reinvention tribe worked on making this book matter

The Chief Reinvention Officer Handbook: How to Thrive in Chaos was co-created, tested, and improved by a community of true business leaders, change-makers, strategy consultants, innovation practitioners, and pioneers. We are deeply grateful to our tribe of over 3,000 practitioners from more than 40 countries who participated in our workshops, surveys, and tool-testing efforts. And some went above and beyond crafting, editing, and contributing to these pages:

Katarina Aaron, Canada	**Marité Ball,** USA	**Mike Bucher,** Austria	**Elena Chernenko,** Belarus
Nurtay Abilgaliyev, Kazakhstan	**Michelle Bartlett,** United Kingdom	**Svitlana Buko,** Russia, Slovenia, & Italy	**Dmitry Chernenko,** Belarus
Shelagh Aitken, United Kingdom	**Maia Beatty,** USA	**Anna Bulaeva,** Russia	**Lisa Chernenko,** Belarus & Russia
Damla Aktan, Turkey	**Christopher Bishop,** USA	**Violeta Bulc,** Slovenia	**Dave Cherry,** USA
Stefan Alijevikj, Macedonia	**J.R. Bjerklie,** USA	**Simon Butt-Bethlendy,** United Kingdom	**Dusan Cicmil,** Slovenia
Agustin Andrade, Argentina	**Madelyn Blair,** USA	**Fernando Caballero,** Peru	**Kandy Cleland,** USA
Sonja Angelovska, Macedonia	**Lucie Blais,** Canada	**Pablo Calvo,** Mexico	**Damon Colaluca,** USA
Ivan Antonijevic, Montenegro	**Jorge Blanco,** Mexico	**Monica Calzolari,** USA	**Joe Cristiano,** Canada
Mirza Asfaar Baig, Saudi Arabia	**Krishna Bobba,** USA	**Yuliya Cannon,** USA	**Dan Croitoru,** Romania
Laurent Astaix, France	**Kath Bogie,** USA	**Joan Carbonell,** Spain	**Verushka Cruz,** Australia
Martin Baeuerle, Qatar	**Jessica Brennan,** Belgium	**Jak Carroll,** Australia	**Michael Cullen,** Canada
Cindy Balan, USA	**Ania Brown,** Belarus & USA	**Dave Chamberlain,** Canada	**Paolo Curati,** Italy
Audrey Ball, USA	**Scarlett Brukmann,** Australia	**Alfredo Chavarín Pimentel,** Mexico	**Matthew Cuthbertson,** Australia

Elizabeth Dalling, Israel

Alexandra De Pretis-Elste, Austria

Marc de Sainte Foy, Belgium

Olivier Delattre, France

Sonia Di Maulo, Canada

Silviya Dineva, Bulgaria

Dmitry Dmitriev, Kazakhstan

Patricia Dopazo, USA

Eleni Dracopoulos, Canada

Neil Drobny, USA

Aleksas Drozdovskis, Lithuania & Netherlands

Charl du Bois, South Africa

Eloise Duncan, Canada

Johana Dunlop, France

John Dyckhoff, New Zealand

Anastasia Dyuryagina, Russia

Ozioma Egwuonwu, USA

Michael Emmart, USA

Mary Fair-Taylor, USA

Susanna Farnes, Spain

Katja Fasink, Slovenia

Bill Ferguson, USA

Jasmina Ferk, Slovenia

Carlena Ficano, USA

Owen Finn, Ireland

Gil Friend, USA

Laura Galiyeva, Kazakhstan

Dennette Gardner, USA

Marsel Gareev, Russia

Katarina Gašperlin, Slovenia

Christiane Gingras, Canada

Metka Glas, Slovenia

Lambert Gneisz, Austria

Lindsey Godwin, USA

Maja Gorjanc, Slovenia

Živa Gorup Reichmann, Slovenia

Tracey Gould, South Africa

David Gouthro, Canada

Gary Graham, South Africa

Manja Greimeier, Germany

Rini Grover, USA

Eduardo H. Guerra, Mexico

Gillian Haley, USA

William Hancy, USA

Jim Hankins, USA

Gretchen Harnick, USA

Tania Harvey, United Kingdom

Ed Hawkins, USA

Frank Henrich, Germany

Christoph Herold, Germany

Clodagh Higgins, Ireland

Thomas Hinterseer, France

Florence His, France

Georgeta Hisic, Romania

Birgit Hochreiter, Austria

Rinor Hoxha, Albania

Gašper Hren, Slovenia

Raushan Irgaliyeva, Kazakhstan

Ivan Ivanovic, Serbia

Klaudija Javornik, Slovenia

Lila Jernovoi, USA

Vladimir Jernovoi, USA

Gregor Jeromen, Slovenia

Urška Jež, Slovenia

Beata Jiraskova, Slovakia

Zdenka Junasova, Slovakia

Luka Kacil, Slovenia

Hokuma Karimova, Azerbaijan

Olga Kashparova, Russia

Jatin Kataria, India

Marko Ketler, Slovenia

Barbara Khattri, United Kingdom

Gordana Kierans, Croatia

Pierre Kleinhans, South Africa

Sonja Klopcic, Slovenia

François Knuchel, United Kingdom	**Michael Magdalenic,** Belgium	**Susan Mills,** USA	**John Peluso,** USA
Andreja Kodrin, Slovenia	**Martin Maitz,** Austria	**Aleyona Mitina,** Kazakhstan & Austria	**Debra Penzone,** USA
Mitja Kolbe, Slovenia	**Maja Majstorović Hajduković,** Slovenia	**Bernard Mohr,** USA	**Olga Peresild,** Estonia
Krystal Kolodziejak, Canada	**Evgeny Makhina,** Russia	**Pascale Molin,** France	**Nevenka Pergar,** Slovenia
Siniša Košćina, Croatia	**Anurag Maloo,** India	**Debby Montelly,** France	**Erin Perkins,** USA
Greg Krauska, Austria	**Ana Marinič,** Slovenia	**Jose Antonio Morales,** Peru & Slovenia	**Denyse Perry,** USA
Kathy Krone, USA	**Mojca Markizeti,** Slovenia	**Yernar Nakisbekov,** Russia	**Sandy Piderit,** USA
Ina Kukovič Borovnik, Slovenia	**Urs Maron,** Switzerland	**Aizhan Nasibullina,** Kazakhstan	**Tea Podlipnik,** Slovenia
Erin Kurchina, Canada	**Shawn Marshall,** USA	**Alexander Nenashev,** Russia	**Milan Pokrivcak,** Czech Republic
Anna Kuzina, Russia	**Jose Antonio Mateo Moreno,** Spain	**Ha Nguyen,** Russia & Vietnam	**Ales Ponikvar,** Slovenia
Muriel Larvaron, France	**Aidan McCullen,** Ireland	**Carolee Noury,** USA	**Sonya Prasad,** Canada
Shukhrat Latypayev, Kazahkstan	**Megan McDougald,** Canada	**Marjeta Novak,** Slovenia	**Martina Radvakova,** Slovakia
Jennifer Lavoie, USA	**Molly McGuigan,** USA	**Roshon Omar,** South Africa	**Muhd Ibnur Rashad,** Singapore
Rok Lesjak, Slovenia	**Kent McKown,** USA	**Tatiana Orglerova,** Czech Republic	**Gverino Ratosa,** Slovenia
Mark Levy, USA	**Yosr Melki,** Netherlands	**Kristi Buckles Otto,** USA	**Irina Redicheva,** Russia
Antonio Lorente Redondo, Spain	**Jim Merhaut,** USA	**Marin Pahija,** Albania	**Julie Rennecker,** USA
Barbara Luckmann Jagodic, Slovenia	**Migena Merkoci,** Albania	**Mateja Panjan,** Slovenia	**Corry Robertson,** Canada
Pinki Luwaca, South Africa	**Natalya Michurina,** Kazakhstan	**Ignacio Pavez,** Chile	**Helena Roks,** Belgium
Duncan MacLachlan, France	**Dmitry Milchak,** Canada	**Merlin Pearson,** USA	**Tania Rowland,** New Zealand

Cody Royle, Canada

Kelsey Rumburg, USA

Paul Ryabov, Russia

Angus Ryan, South Africa

Katya Salavei Bardos, USA & Belarus

Ryan Y. Samia, USA

Satish Samtani, Canada

Greg Scollon, Canada

Anne Scott-Putney, USA

Mathew Sedze, Ireland

Mirjam Seher, Germany

Iztok Seljak, Slovenia

Klemen Šešok, Slovenia

Saviola Shahollari, Albania

Yerbol Shaimakhanov, Kazakhstan

Prabha Shankar, India

Scott Shelfer, USA

Natalie Shell, Israel

Maryam Shirazian, Canada

Anton Shishov, Russia

Olga Shumkova, Russia

Adriana Sierra Rodriguez, Mexico

Danielle Silverman, Canada

Steve Smith, United Kingdom

Neil Socratous, Australia

Maria Sorokina, Russia

Cristina Spanu, Romania

Victor Spence, Scotland

Mer Stafford, USA

Anna Stepanova, Russia

Robyn Stratton-Berkessel, USA

Alima Sumembayeva, Kazakhstan

Sherri Sutton, USA

Ingela Svedin, Sweden

Alexander Sychev, Russia

Alexandra Sytnik, Kazakhstan

Don Tamelin, Canada

Ziva Tavcar, Switzerland

Maria Fernanda Teixeira da Costa, Brazil

Mainur Tleumbet, Kazakhstan

Cheri Torres, USA

Ian Toruno, Panama

Jane Triplett, USA

Behçet Murat Türen, Turkey

Jurij Urbanec, Slovenia

Matthew Urdan, USA

Ildar Valiullov, Kazakhstan

Jolanda van Heerden, South Africa

Olga Veligurska, Slovenia

Heikki Visnapuu, Estonia

Henrik Vittrup Pedersen, Denmark

Eugene Volkov, Russia

Michael Walsh, Italy & United Kingdom

Pamela Ward, South Africa

Cindy Washabaugh, USA

Robert Wellman, USA

Lea Weyermann Lozar, Switzerland & Slovenia

Kathy Wilkins, Canada

Tim Witherell, USA

Fanaye Wolde-Giorghis, Canada

Colleen Wtorek, Canada

Ildar Yussupov, Kazahkstan

Monica-Elena Zamfir, Poland

Elvira Zhanayeva, Kazakhstan

Julia Zhdanova, Russia

Andrei Zhandrov, Russia

Maria Zhukova, Russia & Slovenia

Ksenija Zorc, Slovenia

We also had amazing thinkers and doers who contributed to the book without realizing it

For instance, one of the many concepts and tools presented in this book is the concept of Titanic Syndrome, which you will get a chance to discover very soon. The first time I saw the Titanic used as a business case was in a customer service class given by **Professor Juan Serrano.** While discussing the 1997 movie, he inspired me to research the ship's story and build connections with business practice. Once my team and I dove into the historical records, we discovered facts and insights we had never seen before. Those facts and insights became the foundation for what I would later call the Titanic Syndrome, one of many ideas inside this book.

The idea of collaboratively writing a book came from the fantastic team behind Business Model Canvas. Their book, *Business Model Generation,* by **Alexander Osterwalder** and **Yves Pigneur,** was co-created by 470 practitioners and inspired us to involve our reinvention community in writing this book together.

Throughout the book, we highlight countless books, articles, theories, and methods that added to our thinking. Professor Yuval Noah Harari made a strong case about using reinvention as a skill to teach our kids in his **2018 Wired article.** Professor John Kotter got us wondering about **the difference between leadership and management,** which paved the way to our concept of a healthy Reinvention Cycle. Professor Everett Rogers' **law of diffusion of innovation,** first introduced in his 1962 book *Diffusion of Innovations,* is at the core of why we choose reinvention (and not innovation!) as the primary method for dealing with change. These are just a few of the giants on whose shoulders this work stands.

Remember: This is a handbook

It is designed to serve you as a practical reference point, a type of resource sometimes called **vade mecum** (Latin, "go with me") or pocket reference. My goal is to provide a wide range of tools to be used in many different situations as your life and business evolve, and the challenges you face change.

You can read it in a sequence provided or decide to jump around from section to section. That's why a simple table of contents would not do.

On the next page, you'll find a mind map of the book in its entirety and decide where you want to start.

We put together material we see as the most useful for your organization in the present moment. Keep in mind, though, that we'll

always have resources, insights, and cases in the pipeline, ready to appear in our virtual bonus vault, which you can always access at **www ChiefReinventionOffice com/resources**

What we offer in the bonu section can change depend ing on your feedback, ou consulting and research e forts, and the world aroun us. If you have a suggestio for something to includ in the bonus vault — say, a ca se or a research question c a discussion of a manage rial dilemma — contact u through our website. We'll tr our best to develop conter around your needs.

Map of contents

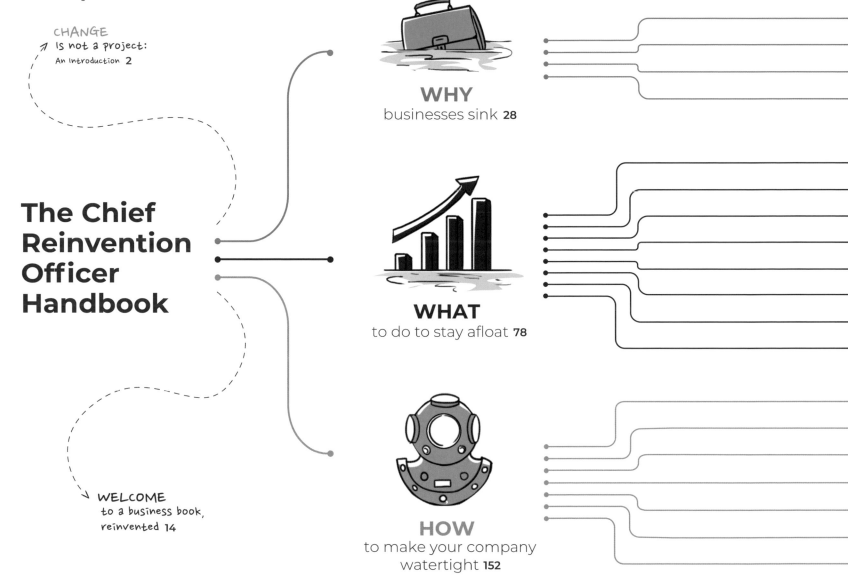

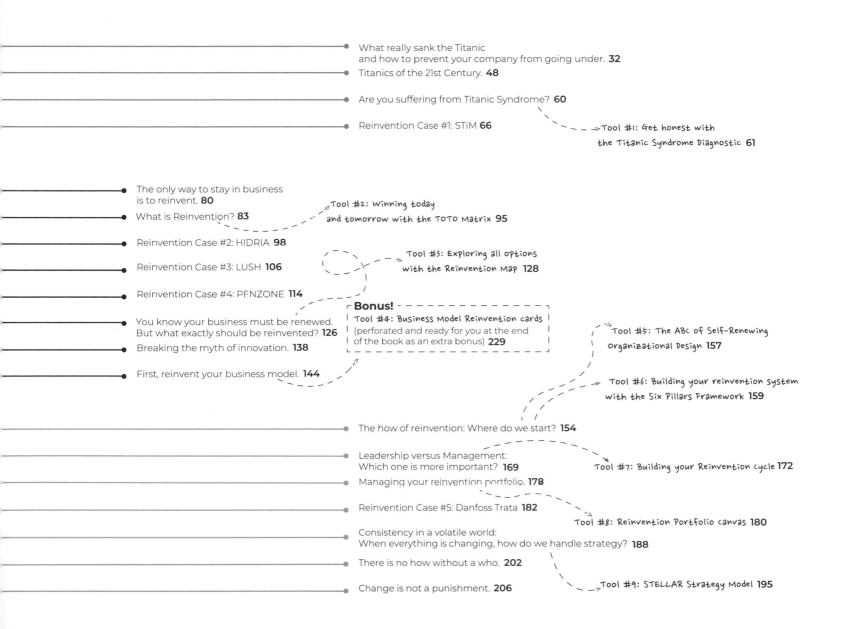

The future is already here —
it's just not very evenly
distributed.

William Gibson

PART 1

WHY

BUSINESSES SINK

Ask any manager or entrepreneur on planet Earth, "What is your key challenge?" You are sure to hear an answer like this over and over again: "Staying afloat!"

The fast-moving, up-and-down economy we live in today makes the task of staying afloat increasingly difficult. Just as we handle one crisis, another appears on the horizon.

Digital, millennials, new regulations, new competition, political turmoil, Artificial Intelligence, Industry 4.0, blockchain, sharing economy, circular economy, substitute products, you name it. The waves of disruption come crashing faster and faster, fundamentally changing the way we work, profit, and compete. How do we survive and even thrive?

The metaphor of staying afloat – the way a sailing boat stays afloat on the raging ocean – offers a perfect answer to all of us looking for an answer. A sailing boat does not fight the waters or try to avoid the wind. Instead, it uses the power of water and air to move with purpose. It not only survives, but also thrives on turbulence, making wind its friend. But to do that, we have to make sure that the boat is built correctly, the crew is trained properly, and the right maps, binoculars, and compasses are at our disposal.

That is why we use the story of a ship as the central theme of this book. It is an invitation to think of yourself, your team, and your organization in a new way. The key question is not how we survive until the storm is over. The key question is how we learn to use the storm to power up our sails. And for that, we have to start by understanding and embracing the storm.

> ## " How do we survive — and even thrive?

What trends, changes, and disruptions are most important for you and your business? What keeps you up at night? What gets you excited?

WHAT REALLY SANK THE TITANIC AND HOW TO PREVENT YOUR COMPANY FROM GOING UNDER

For nearly twenty years, we've been working in the field of survival and sustainability — researching and developing ways for businesses to stay afloat, no matter what disruptions come their way. To understand the mechanics of survival, it helps to look at the successes and failures of the past.

One of the best known and most illustrative failures of all time? The Titanic.

On a chilly Sunday night, April 14, 1912, at 11:49 pm, the Royal Mail Steamer Titanic, en route from Southampton to New York, collided with an iceberg and sank within three hours, leading to the deaths of nearly 1,514 of the 2,224 passengers and crew. The ship's story is both famous and powerful as it holds lessons to be learned on how to create and prevent disasters.

The largest man-made moving object at the time, the Titanic was considered unsinkable by all: experts, media, and the public. The ship was equipped with the most advanced naval technology available, as well as a remarkable crew of some of the most experienced and respected naval leaders of their time. So the crucial question is: Why did the Titanic sink?

> **The crucial question is: Why did the Titanic sink?**

What, in your view, sank the Titanic? Don't worry if you haven't studied the history of this disaster; the famous movie is a solid reference as it has been confirmed to be historically accurate and will do for the purpose of this exercise.

Write down whatever easily comes to mind:

Warnings

Most of us know that the Titanic's crew was aware of the dangerous icebergs in the area. But some of us don't realize how many times the crew was warned. The answer: at least six times! The last and most specific of the six was not passed along to the captain by senior radio operator John George "Jack" Phillips because it was not marked with the prefix "MSG" (Masters' Service Gram), which requires a personal acknowledgement from the captain. Phillips interpreted the message as not urgent and returned to sending messages for the first-class passengers to a receiver on shore at Cape Race, Newfoundland, before the ship went out of range.

Even more: Before the Titanic hit the iceberg, Phillips was so concerned with keeping the high-paying customers satisfied that when interrupted with a warning of the upcoming ice field, he told Cyril Evans, the radio operator of the passing ship Californian, "Shut up, shut up, I am busy; I am working, Cape Race!" Customer satisfaction is all the rage. But pushing it for the wrong whim of every customer might accidentally push your business over the edge.

Unless the job requires constant customer contact, chances are your employees have near-zero interaction with customers and their needs. When it comes to suppliers, the situation is even worse: Unless you are a buyer, most believe it is the job of the procurement department to get insights and warnings from suppliers.

Yet it is precisely the regular and deliberate connection with customers and suppliers that offers you rich insights and timely warnings of a possible crisis to be averted. Having most of the employees cut off from the external partners creates real danger and increases the chance of missed opportunities.

> **Customer satisfaction is all the rage. But pushing it for the wrong whim of every customer might accidentally push your business over the edge.**

How often do you get insights, trends, and warnings from your customers and suppliers?
What can you and your team do to get better and more timely warnings?

No practice

The Titanic's final voyage was also its very first. In fact, the ship barely made it out of the construction site and had only a few hours of test runs in open waters before sailing across the ocean. Neither ship nor crew had significant time to "gel" together, and the most vital performance and safety procedures were never practiced.

The ship's mandatory sea trials began at 6 a.m. on Tuesday, April 2, 1912, only two days after all final fittings were completed and barely eight days before it was due to leave Southampton on its maiden voyage. Over the course of about twelve hours, the Titanic was navigated at different speeds, first in a protected area and then in open waters. The ship's turning ability was tested, and a "crash stop" was practiced. The Titanic was able to come to a full stop in 850 yards (777 meters) or 195 seconds. Twelve days later it would take the Titanic about thirty-seven seconds from the moment the iceberg was sighted to the moment the ship collided with it. When reality hit, it hit the Titanic hard and fast.

Even more disturbing is that absolutely no safety drills were ever organized before or during the voyage, and no one among leadership was in charge of passenger safety. In an ironic twist of fate, the first lifeboat drill for passengers and crew was scheduled for 11 a.m. on the day of the ship's sinking. However, the captain canceled it with no explanation just hours before the collision. As a result, the crew had no idea how to act in a disaster.

No procedures were developed, and no skills were built for operating lifeboat equipment.

No clear passenger communication and organization protocol was designed or taught to the crew.

Cost of no practice? Even though the ship carried about 2,224 people, it had only lifeboats for 1,200. With no practice for lifeboat operations, the crew deployed many boats half-empty, and as a result, no more than 710 people were saved.

Just like any other competence, managing change can be learned and developed into a strong managerial muscle. The problem is that most of us in business are expected to perform improvisationally: We never hold "practice meetings" or give teams a few weeks of "rehearsals time" before the project commences. When it comes to managing change, the situation is more dire: When building our businesses, we have a bias toward stability. Most companies are built with an assumption that the situation will remain stable and predictable with a relatively low volatility.

Take the budgeting process, for example. For a typical publicly traded company, the budget is set once a year, and adjustments are made quarterly. But what happens when markets get dangerously volatile or a global pandemic hits?

We recently worked with a global 70,000+ employee commodity company that experienced a nearly 80% drop in prices for its signature product. The company had absolutely no way to reconcile this difference quickly. Its formal re-budgeting would take months, and by then the damage could have been irreversible. When it comes to change, practice is crucial.

" **Just like any other competence, managing change can be learned. For that, practice is crucial.**

How does your company cultivate change and reinvention capacity in its people and managerial processes? What works? What can be improved?

Past success

On the night of the collision, the ship's captain had already gone to bed. First Officer William McMaster Murdoch was left in charge of the ship. At age thirty-nine, Murdoch had sixteen years of maritime experience behind him and was known for his "cool head, quick thinking, and professional judgement." In fact, Murdoch was particularly famous for his masterful track record of averting ship collisions.

In one instance, Second Officer Murdoch of a new liner, the Arabic, averted a disaster when a passing ship was spotted bearing down on the Arabic out of the darkness. Murdock overrode a command from his superior to steer the ship to the left, rushing into the wheelhouse, pushing the quartermaster to a side and holding the ship steady on course. As a result, the two ships passed within inches of one another without any damage.

The incident with the Arabic was one of many that Murdoch mastered in his career, and in the thirty-seven seconds between the first sighting of the iceberg and its collision with the Titanic, the officer fully relied on successes of the past to make executive decisions in the present. We all know how it turned out.

While practice is crucial to work out the details, it is essential to use past experience deliberately and intelligently. Practice gets you prepared but can quickly turn into overconfidence or refusal to change. Companies large and small have a love affair with the mantra "We've always done it this way." However, as a slew of research summarized by Fast Company suggests, past experience can be deceiving and dangerous: "It's important for leaders to understand their teams' tendency to overgeneralize from past experience. Just because one product launch went well doesn't mean the same approach will work equally well for the next one."

Marshall Goldsmith and Mark Reiter in their bestseller, *What Got You Here Won't Get You There,* paint a clear picture of how past successes limit our ability to deal with new challenges: "We get positive reinforcement from our past successes, and, in a mental leap that's easy to justify, we think that our past success is predictive of great things in our future... Our delusions become a serious liability when we need to change. We sit there with the godlike feelings, and when someone tries to make us change, we regard them with unadulterated bafflement."

> **What got you here will not get you there. Instead, your past success might actually destroy your every dream.**

Where do you see past experience serving your company well, and where is it limiting progress? What can you do to become more mindful and selective in the use of past experience?

No binoculars

The night of the collision was clear and still. Perched 50 feet (15 meters) above the forecastle deck in a small open box called "the crow's nest," lookouts Frederick Fleet and Reginald Lee worked their two-hour shift. Inside the nest, Fleet and Lee had a large bell to grab general attention and a telephone to reach the captain's bridge. What they did not have, however, was a pair of binoculars.

A company's ability to notice and adapt to change is often seen as an issue of motivation and commitment. Motivation is important, but it can take you only so far. No matter how motivated and committed to success your people are, if they don't have "binoculars" — the tools they need to deliver — your efforts are useless. User-friendly technology, solid assets, smart business processes, and well-oiled management systems must be at the fingertips of employees to be able to perform when it matters the most.

One hundred years later, with all the advances in modern technology, it is still hard to imagine any ship in the open waters with no binoculars. The Titanic, too, had a number of binoculars on board, but for much of the trip they were locked up in a storage cabinet.

The key was held by Second Officer David Blair, who, in a last-minute leadership change decision, was asked to sit out the trip before the ship's departure from Southampton on April 9. Leaving the Titanic at the last minute and very disappointed, Blair forgot to hand the key to his replacement. It is likely that the cabinet or its lock could be broken. However, nobody made the call.

For your business, what tools are crucial today? How can your company make sure that everyone has these crucial tools at the right time in this changing environment?

Lookout Fred Fleet, who survived the Titanic disaster, would later insist that if binoculars had been available, the iceberg would have been spotted in enough time for the ship to take evasive action. The use of binoculars would have given "enough time to get out of the way," Fleet reportedly said.

By the time the iceberg was noticed, the ship was too close to avert the disaster.

This was, quite literally, the case of blinding overconfidence.

The binoculars story also highlights that major leadership decisions were made while the Titanic was already in progress. David Blair was one of the top three executives in charge of the ship when it left for its maiden voyage. However, he was asked to step down and had to leave the ship during its first stop, taking the key to the binoculars cabinet with him.

Moving people the same way you move furniture, without full understanding of their scope of responsibility, is a recipe for disaster.

> **" This was, quite literally, the case of blinding overconfidence.**

In your company, how are leadership and team decisions made? What can you do to strengthen the capacity of your teams to be ready for unexpected change?

The iceberg

We already reviewed a number of possible causes for the Titanic disaster, but we may not have come to the one you probably wrote down first: the iceberg.

Whenever we work with a company or discuss the Titanic story on stage, the iceberg is among the first causes mentioned. And if you go back a few pages and review your own list of the possible causes, chances are the iceberg is among the main ones.

So why did we leave the most obvious for last?

Most of the time when we are asked to work with a company on reinventing its products, processes, or the entire business model, we are not there during the good times. By the time we are called,

things are already deteriorating: The iceberg has been hit, so to speak. And oh boy, it is easy to blame that iceberg!

The iceberg can take many forms. Sneaky competitors, overbearing regulators, lousy weather, bad design, late suppliers, lazy customers, those finance-department knuckleheads: We've heard it all. It is so easy to blame your predicament on someone else. But here is the thing: While you cannot prevent the iceberg from appearing, you can damn well make sure you don't hit it. The choice is in your hands.

> **While you cannot prevent the iceberg from appearing, you can damn well make sure you don't hit it. The choice is in your hands.**

The sea and the sky

Finally, there are two more "suspects" in the Titanic story that often get forgotten: the sea and the sky.

As you remember from your school days, ocean and air work together as a part of the water cycle, much the way the different forces in our business environment work together to form new storms or calm the waters for our company. When it comes to literal or metaphorical Titanics, there is no question that the sea and the sky always play a role.

If it were not for the movement of the water and the wind, the iceberg and the ship would not have encountered each other on that fatal night in the North Atlantic Ocean. Similarly, without a wide range of interconnected forces — technological, eco-nomic, social, political, eco-logical, and much more — our companies would not have to face many of the disruptions and crises we do today. It seems that lately, the sea and the sky that our business-es aim to navigate are turning increasingly more chaotic.

At the beginning of the book, I spoke about the rate of change and the constant disruption we are all experiencing. Let me add a few strokes to that picture: 2017 PWC survey of CEOs conclud-ed that crises are hitting with greater frequency, with 15% of CEOs facing five or more crises in the past three years and 30% anticipating more than one crisis in the follow-ing three years, including fi-nancial, legal, technological, operational, humanitarian, reputational, and human cap-ital disruptions. By the end of those three years, the fears seemed well-justified: In the 2020 survey, the share of busi-ness leaders very confident in their twelve-month growth prospects fell to 27%, the low-est level since 2009.

> **It seems that lately, the sea and the sky that our businesses aim to navigate are turning increasingly more chaotic.**

How can we not only survive, but also thrive in this chaos?

To answer this question, we must first understand the nature of chaos. What comes to your mind when you hear the word?

In the spring of 2020, I asked more than 700 students of our Reinvention Academy — all business managers, owners or consultants — this very question. "What comes to mind when you hear the word *chaos?*"

The answers were incredibly consistent: disorganization, anarchy, loss of control, craziness, darkness, mess, horror. One answer stood above all: lack of order.

Yet when you pose the same question to scientists, they paint a completely different picture. Look up chaos across the wide range of scientific publications, and you'll see that as mathematicians Jonathan Borwein and Michael Rose put it, "Order and chaos are not always diametrically opposed. Chaotic systems are an intimate mix of the two: From the outside they display unpredictable and chaotic behavior, but expose the inner workings, and you discover a perfectly deterministic set of equations ticking like clockwork."

You will also discover Margaret Wheatley, who in her classic book *Leadership and the New Science: Discovering Order in a Chaotic World* explains the relationship between chaos and order in this way: "These two forces are now understood as mirror images, two states that contain the other. A system can descend into chaos and unpredictability, yet within that state of chaos the system is held within boundaries that are well-ordered and predictable. Without the partnering of these two great forces, no change or progress is possible. Chaos is necessary to new creative ordering."

Perhaps the best illustration of what chaos is that I ever saw came from geneticist Bruce Lipton at one of his lectures about three years ago.

Remember the last time you were at a busy rail station like the Grand Central in New York. Imagine you are standing on the balcony looking down. You see hundreds of people moving in different directions, wedding pictures being taken, and people waiting to meet their loved ones.

It seems like a lack of order, but it's not. This is actually chaos. The reason is that everyone in this picture is not moving mindlessly or randomly. Everyone has a purpose, a direction, a logic for their actions.

> **How can we not only survive chaos — but learn to thrive in it?**

What would lack of order look like? If I get a megaphone and scream "Fire!," people will panic and run with no purpose or clear direction. That would be disorder indeed, but it has nothing to do with chaos.

Chaos is not a lack of order. Chaos is a presence of more than one order. Chaos is having some of your customers yearning for a new car while others are seeing car ownership as "something boomers do," and you still need to find a way to satisfy both. Chaos is having some of your suppliers betting with one type of technology and others choosing an alternative, and you still need to work with both. Chaos is noticing one country's regulation is a complete opposite from another, and your company's policy still needs to find room for both. Chaos is a natural state of any complex system, the kind we are living and working in today. And understanding this gives you power to use chaos the way a sail uses the wind as a new and emerging reality rather than running or hiding from it.

❝ **Chaos is not a lack of order. Chaos is a presence of more than one order.**

TITANICS OF THE TWENTY-FIRST CENTURY

We've already talked about a number of the problems that helped sink the Titanic, but there were many others that we haven't yet mentioned. The quality of the metal that held the walls together was questionable. The construction was rushed. The ship was traveling at high speed despite repeated ice warnings.

But of all these things that went wrong, there was one problem that was more important than all the others: **the arrogance and overconfidence in past success.** The blind trust of the status quo. The absolute, often unconscious belief that what works now will continue to work indefinitely. The numbing assumption that things will stay the same. The love affair with our existing way of life, our products, our ways, our ships.

Embedded in every aspect of the Titanic operations was the assumption of the ship's mighty power. In the eyes of everyone involved, it was untouchable, unbreakable, and unsinkable. For a ship perceived as "too big to fail," no vigilance was necessary, no preparation for a possible disruption was required, and no technology for crisis management was assured. The team became overconfident and complacent. Unsinkable led to the unthinkable.

The story of the Titanic is one of the most known and recognized worldwide, so it is hard to imagine that it can repeat itself. Yet every year with remarkable consistency we see companies large and small calling "SOS" amid serious business crisis. In fact, you might be surprised how many companies end up getting acquired, declaring bankruptcy, or worse — never recovering — in the process. One statistic best illustrates the low survival rate of "unsinkable titans of business": Of the 500 mighty companies originally included on the Fortune 500 list in 1955, only 60 survive today. That is a sinking rate of 88%.

Take, for example, the most known "Titanics" of the twenty-first century: Kodak and

> ## "Unsinkable led to the unthinkable.

Nokia. Kodak had been the staple of American culture throughout the twentieth century, selling at one point 90% of all photographic film and 85% of all cameras in the United States. Nokia had been the number one cell phone seller from 1998 to 2007, controlling at its prime 40% of the entire global handset market. Yet Kodak filed for bankruptcy in 2012, while Nokia was forced to sell its mobile devices business to Microsoft in 2013 to save itself from its own collapse.

Both companies had to use their "shipwrecks" to rebuild from the ground up, taking years to find a new footing.

The story of the Titanic is the most powerful example of a "too big to fail" mindset. Our friends at Kodak and Nokia suffered from the same disease: The sheer size of the companies created an illusion of being untouchable and unsinkable. Enron, Lehman Brothers, Blockbuster, Toys R Us, Borders, and Myspace all went through the same disenchantment of blind belief in their own ability to withstand any storm or disruption.

Blockbuster, for example, at its peak in 2004, employed more than 60,000 people at its 9,000 stores.

When Dish Network bought the bankrupt Blockbuster in 2011, it was staying afloat with only 1,700 stores remaining. But it did not have to go that way. Greg Sattel of Forbes explains:

"In 2000, Reed Hastings, the founder of a fledgling company called Netflix, flew to Dallas to propose a partnership to Blockbuster CEO John Antioco and his team. The idea was that Netflix would run Blockbuster's brand online, and Antioco's firm would promote Netflix in its stores. Hastings got laughed out of the room. We all know what happened next."

The Titanic Syndrome has sunk many companies. This is why it is time for us to meet this enemy. Titanic Syndrome: a corporate disease in which organizations facing disruption bring about their own downfall through arrogance, excessive attachment to past success, or inability recognize and adapt to the new and emerging reality.

What does Titanic Syndrome look like?

In meetings, discussions, and decisions, people throughout the "infected" company show explicit or implicit assumptions of superiority, untouchability, and unsinkability. At a personal level, this shows up as an overwhelming belief that success of the past will guarantee achievement in the future.

It also shows up when we rely blindly on our own past experience. We all love a great success story. Getting it right, making things work, and achieving success are in the very DNA of modern life. However, when things change abruptly, your own past success might quickly become your greatest enemy. What worked yesterday might destroy you today. What got you here will not get you there. Instead, it might actually sabotage your every dream.

Some companies develop Titanic Syndrome not via arrogance or strong attachment to past success, but through pure inability to recognize that things might change suddenly. All of us are creatures of habit, and it is so tempting to think that things will stay as they are. For such companies the idea that things that worked before no longer work comes out of nowhere — blinding and paralyzing everyone along the way. Disaster follows.

“ **Titanic Syndrome: a corporate disease in which organizations facing disruption bring about their own downfall through arrogance, excessive attachment to past success, or inability to recognize the new and emerging reality.**

Why Titanic Syndrome is more dangerous to business today than ever

Once upon a time, our companies enjoyed long and healthy lives, with a slow rise to the top of financial performance and a gradual decline to annihilation. The rate of change was so slow that it was easy to develop Titanic Syndrome and still survive. We had all the time in the world to renew our business on our terms. If a new "iceberg" showed up on the horizon – a new competitor, a new technology, a new regulation – your company could adapt slowly and even get to enjoy the ride.

But that fairy tale is long gone.

As I mentioned in this handbook's introduction, Steve Denning of Forbes paints this picture perfectly:"Fifty years ago, 'milking the cash cow' could go on for many decades. What's different today is that globalization and the shift in power in the marketplace from buyer to seller is dramatically shortening the life expectancy of firms that are merely milking their cash cows. Half a century ago, the life expectancy of a firm in the Fortune 500 was around **seventy-five** years. Now it's **less than fifteen** years and declining even further."

Denning's claims are supported by research published by Richard Foster and Sarah Kaplan in 2001, which documented how corporate life cycles were diminishing rapidly. Yet much has happened since 2001.

The increasing level of globalization, showcased so painfully during the 2008-2009 global economic crisis, powered by the ever-increasing access to knowledge (think Google, free online courses, Khan Academy, etc.), means that more of us are inventing every day and sharing those inventions globally than ever before. There is more startup activity today than ever before, but those startups also continue to die at a high rate: Only one-third survive to the ten-year mark.

With all these pressures, the demand for corporate (economic, communal, and personal) reinvention has grown even more.

Does it mean that we are all doomed? Absolutely not!

What separates companies that survive from those that perish is **the ability to start a new life cycle.**

Winners are able to pivot their company far enough from the path of destruction to find a new opportunity for growth before stagnation and decline set in.

Timing is so crucial. And if before you had decades to reach the prime, today you might have only a few years.

How many, exactly?

To answer this question, we have launched a global reinvention survey.

In 2018, more than 2,000 participants took part in this research.

The 2020 study is still unfolding, but with the first 1,000 submissions already in, the results are more than telling.

We see how often it is necessary to reinvent, what kind of reinvention is happening, and where opportunities for improvements and breakthroughs are for you today.

Most importantly, the data can show you if you are allocating enough resources for reinvention, approaching it the right way, and reaping the benefits as a result.

These facts are your friends. The data is here to help you make better decisions, and we are ready to share the results. And you can always find the most up-to-date information and analysis among the handbook's online bonus materials at

www.ChiefReinvention Officer.com/resources

1. The speed of change is accelerating

We started this research project in 2018 in an effort to understand how often we need to reinvent to survive and thrive in to-day's business environment. We thought the first results showed a fast-moving world, but the 2020 data is even more telling!

How often do you need to reinvent your company to survive and thrive?

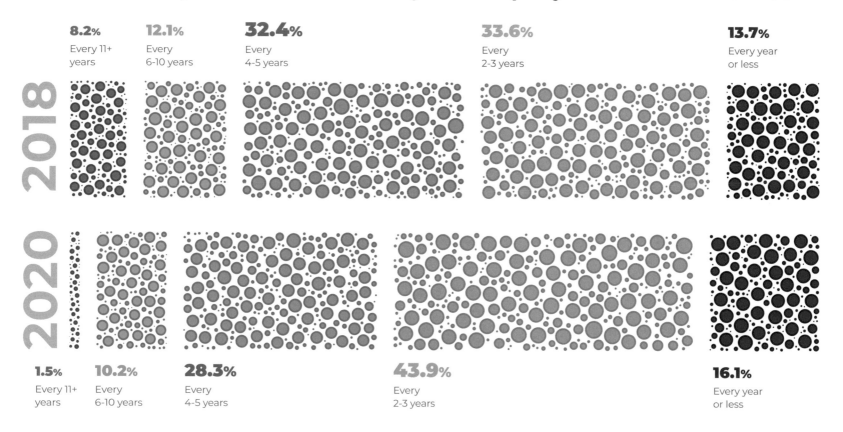

2018

8.2% Every 11+ years

12.1% Every 6-10 years

32.4% Every 4-5 years

33.6% Every 2-3 years

13.7% Every year or less

2020

1.5% Every 11+ years

10.2% Every 6-10 years

28.3% Every 4-5 years

43.9% Every 2-3 years

16.1% Every year or less

2. To survive today, you need to reinvent every 3 years

In 2018, out of over 2,000 managers participating, 47% reported that in order to survive, they needed to reinvent their businesses every three years or less. Data from 2020 is still coming in, but the first 1,000 respondents show that the number has jumped to a whopping 60%.

The median fell at precisely **3 years** – the speed we have not seen in data before.

This means that barely two or three years into your existing business reality, you must start the reinvention process anew — again and again, in a continuous cycle of renewal.

The business you are in today cannot be the business you'll be in three years from now. By then, you will be either entering your new business or heading toward extinction. Period.

years or less

3. There is a much greater need for reinvention

In 2018, despite the reported speed of change, not all industries saw reinvention as a strategic priority. As a result, many got disrupted by start-up newcomers, including the entertainment industry that got shaken up by the likes of Hulu and Amazon Prime, or retail, which is going hrough a fundamental shake-up.

In 2020, there is still variation, but the need for reinvention jumped up across the board. Two scenarios should matter for you:

1. If your industry is prioritizing reinvention, but your company does not, you are at risk of losing to your existing competitors.

2. If your industry is downgrading the need for reinvention, it is at risk of being taken over by startup newcomers. However, this offers a unique opportunity for your company to stand out.

Either way, it is time to face reality and start moving.

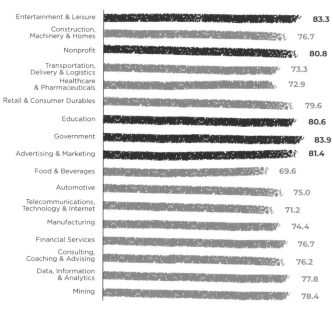

Assessment on a scale of 0-100

- **0-59** Low-to-moderate need for reinvention
- **6079** Considerable need for reinvention
- **80-100** Very high need for reinvention

2018

Entertainment & Leisure	40.8
Construction, Machinery & Homes	44.2
Nonprofit	48.8
Transportation, Delivery & Logistics	49.7
Healthcare & Pharmaceuticals	50.3
Retail & Consumer Durables	50.9
Education	51.6
Government	52.3
Advertising & Marketing	52.3
Food & Beverages	54.7
Automotive	55.0
Telecommunications, Technology & Internet	56.4
Manufacturing	59.9
Financial Services	62.0
Consulting, Coaching & Advising	62.0
Data, Information & Analytics	65.3
Mining	65.6

2020

Entertainment & Leisure	83.3
Construction, Machinery & Homes	76.7
Nonprofit	80.8
Transportation, Delivery & Logistics	73.3
Healthcare & Pharmaceuticals	72.9
Retail & Consumer Durables	79.6
Education	80.6
Government	83.9
Advertising & Marketing	81.4
Food & Beverages	69.6
Automotive	75.0
Telecommunications, Technology & Internet	71.2
Manufacturing	74.4
Financial Services	76.7
Consulting, Coaching & Advising	76.2
Data, Information & Analytics	77.8
Mining	78.4

4. But when it comes to reinvention, companies talk the talk but don't walk the walk

We asked companies to grade themselves on how committed they are to reinvention, how sufficient the resources they are allocating to continuous renewal, how systematic, deliberate and organized they are with their reinvention efforts, and how efficient they are when implementing change initiatives. The answers are clear: words and actions do not match. As a result, efficiency suffers.

1. Commitment
We are committed or extremely committed to reinvention

63.5%

2. Resources
The resources allocated by our company to execute necessary reinvention are low or not at all sufficient

64.1%

4. Efficiency
Our organization is somewhat or not at all effective in anticipating, designing, and implementing reinvention initiatives

64.9%

3. Systematic approach
Our company's reinvention efforts lack system or process for making it happen deliberately and proactively

74.8%

5. It's time to think bigger and bolder

As the intensity of change is increasing and the need for reinvention growing by double digits, it's important to balance incremental efforts (such as continuous improvement) with more radical systemic changes (such as disruptive innovation).

Such balance cannot be static - it must dynamically adjust to the realities on the ground. When a product, an organization, or an entire community reaches the peak of the existing life cycle, a need for radical, disruptive change increases. Once the leap to the new life cycle is made, more incremental improvements are necessary.

Most of the change happening today, however, does not yet follow such a pattern. We asked managers around the world what kind of reinven-tion they experienced most in the past three years **(incremental, intermediate,** or **radical).** We also asked them to share what was reinvented most of the time - just **a part of a system** (for example, just a transmission of a car), **the entire system** (change of the entire car concept), or reinvention of **an entire ecosystem** (in the automotive example, that would include rethink of gas stations, re-do of the supplier system, etc).

The results are clear: the absolute majority of time we focus on small reinventions of small parts of the ecosystem.

That stands in stark contrast to the responses given about the speed of change and the need for reinvention. Businesses around the world report a great need for reinvention - but seem to play small, taking only small steps and reinventing only limited parts of a system. There are plenty of times in the life of a product, a company, or an industry, where such choice is justified - but in 2020 when this research is done, while the entire world is shaken by the global pandemic, incremental reinventions are equivalent to moving the proverbial chairs on the sinking Titanic.

Time to think bigger: ride the waves of change, rather than get crushed by them!

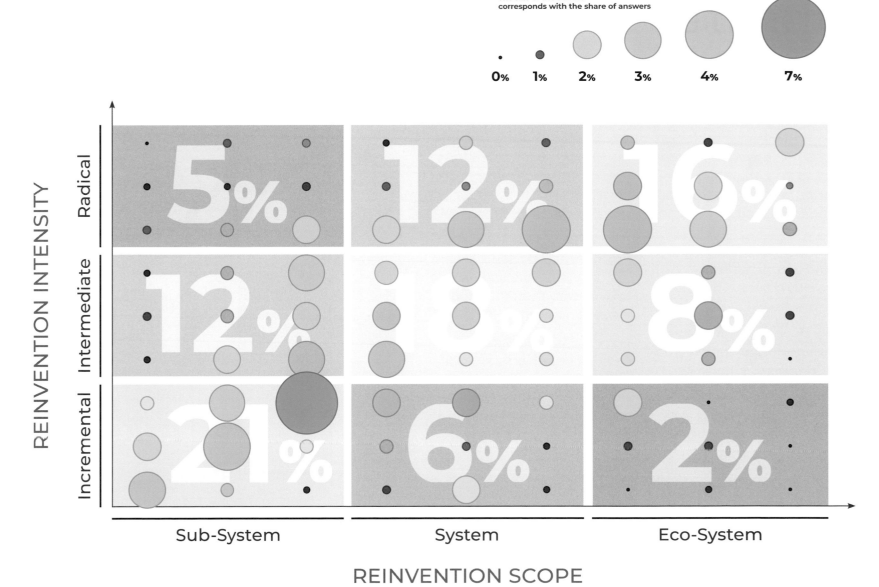

The size of the bubble corresponds with the share of answers

0%   1%   2%   3%   4%   7%

REINVENTION INTENSITY

Radical — Sub-System 5% — System 12% — Eco-System 16%

Intermediate — Sub-System 12% — System 10% — Eco-System 8%

Incremental — Sub-System 21% — System 6% — Eco-System 2%

REINVENTION SCOPE

Sub-System   System   Eco-System

Are you suffering from Titanic Syndrome?

You know that Titanic Syndrome destroyed many companies and careers. You see that it's becoming particularly dangerous today — when the winds of change are blowing stronger and the icebergs show up more and more often. But how do you know if you are ready?

How do you protect yourself and your organization from the dangerous hands of Titanic Syndrome?

How do you diagnose and cure it today — and make sure to prevent it tomorrow?

To answer these questions, we've used insights from key research and added a heavy dose of testing to develop our own Titanic Syndrome Diagnostic. Thousands of people have used it to date and hundreds of organizations (for-profit and non-profit) have been able to start crucial transformations with this tool.

I myself use it regularly in both business and personal life as Titanic Syndrome sneaks up on me even though I should always know better.

Have the tool handy and run this test regularly by yourself, with your team, and across the entire organization to open honest dialogue and lay a foundation for needed action.

Get honest with the Titanic Syndrome Diagnostic

Tool #1

Read each statement below. On the scale from 0 to 5, zero being "This is nothing like our company," and five being "This is 100% our company", assess the relevance of each statement for your organization.

ANTICIPATING CHANGE

Our company gets insights and warnings **from the same sources** (for example, suppliers, customers, professional magazines, etc.) and **rarely** goes out of its comfort zone in soliciting information from unusual sources.

0   1   2   3   4   5

Other employees and I are **rarely asked to share** insights and reflections on potential threats, disruptions or opportunities to our business.

0   1   2   3   4   5

When our company gets insights and warnings about potential disruptions, they are shared with a **small group of people.**

0   1   2   3   4   5

In our company we usually start **reacting** when we are pressed by an unfolding crisis, rather than **anticipate** possible threat or opportunity and respond **proactively.**

0   1   2   3   4   5

We **don't take enough time** for reflection, strategizing, creative thinking, and proactive action.

0   1   2   3   4   5

DESIGNING CHANGE

I **regularly** hear "We have always done it this way" and "That's just the way we do it here" when discussing change at company meetings.

0   1   2   3   4   5

Most people in our company **get angry and frustrated** with the need to do something differently, even if it is for the better.

0   1   2   3   4   5

In our company, leaders often **justify their decisions using past experience as the main argument.** For example: "Trust me, I've done it a million times" or "We tried it this way already, and it will never work."

0   1   2   3   4   5

When we fail, our company often places blame on somebody **on the outside** (competitors, suppliers, government, consumers).

0   1   2   3   4   5

In our organization, changes are made by a small group of people. **Employees rarely get an opportunity to actively engage in developing and deciding on** the new products, processes, and strategies - and learn about decisions at the time of rollout.

0   1   2   3   4   5

IMPLEMENTING CHANGE

I **have not received any training or instruction** for how to start and implement change in our company. I (and most likely many others) are not sure what the procedure is if I want to introduce change.

0   1   2   3   4   5

There are significant gaps between **what we say** about our company's commitment to change and **how we actually work,** allocate our resources, spend our time at meetings, award bonuses, etc.

0   1   2   3   4   5

In our company, we **do not welcome** "practice rounds" or experimentations. Instead, we are expected to execute all change perfectly and are **punished for mistakes and failures.**

0   1   2   3   4   5

During the process of change, we **rarely** stop to celebrate small or short-term wins. Often, **we feel demotivated** and cannot see the progress we are making.

0   1   2   3   4   5

The way our company is organized **makes it difficult to react to change quickly.** For example, our budgeting process is very bureaucratic, making it hard to introduce change in the middle of the year, or our production and investment decisions lock us into a product for years with no easy way to change.

0   1   2   3   4   5

How is your company doing?

Sum up all numbers circled and put the total here:

GUIDE TO SCORES

56-75	36-55	16-35	0-15
Man the lifeboats! You have Titanic Syndrome	Significant signs of Titanic Syndrome	Reasonable change and reinvention skills, with a growing risk for Titanic Syndrome	Excellent change and reinvention skills

What do you need to work on the most?

Sum up all numbers for each category and put the totals into boxes below:

ANTICIPATING CHANGE

DESIGNING CHANGE

IMPLEMENTING CHANGE

With your diagnostic results in hand, the question becomes: What do you do?

Whether you scored high or low, whether you are perfectly equipped to manage any kind of business disaster or your company is suffering from a full-fledged case of Titanic Syndrome — there is something you can do right now to get yourself even more prepared for this era of volatile business:

WHY

Start a conversation on **WHY** Titanic Syndrome is taking over our businesses today. Hold a coffee-and-doughnuts meeting on why businesses are at greater risk of sinking today than ever before. Bring results of our study to your meetings to foster greater understanding of hidden trends that quietly shape our twenty-first century reality.

Survival is not an individual sport. This kind of collective dialogue helps you bring potential problems to the surface, develops a common language, and makes your company much more prepared to address any kind of iceberg heading your way.

WHAT

Equip yourself with specific strategies and solutions on **WHAT** to do to stay afloat. What does successful reinvention look like? What examples can you explore and learn from? What should be done specifically to prepare for the era of endless disruptions?

The second part of this book deals with this topic. Make sure you do the exercises offered at the end of all cases, engage with the frameworks, and explore all twenty-five business model options to choose from.

HOW

Build your own toolbox around **HOW** to make your company watertight: specifically, how you transform your company into an adaptive, ever-evolving powerhouse ready to face any disruption and transform it into a business opportunity.

The third part of the book will offer insights on this subject. We'll focus on the six essential pillars of reinvention as a system — and offer a new canvas for implementing a consistent strategy in the age of extreme uncertainty.

The greatest danger in times of turbulence is not the turbulence, it is to act with yesterday's logic.

Peter Drucker

Reinvention case #1

STiM

What comes to mind when you hear "a lifesaving job"?

A doctor? A nurse? A firefighter ? Perhaps an occasional cancer treatment researcher?

Whatever your list might be, I am ready to make one bet: It does not contain a road-marking professional. (Yes, I mean all those people who design, build, and operate machines that put safety marks on our roads.)

We take road markings for granted. Yet invention and constant reinvention of the road-marking technology is responsible for literally millions of lives saved from accidents. Study after study shows the incredible impact of even a partial road marking.

For example, 1959 research showed that adding simple edge lines on rural two-lane routes with minimum average traffic of 1,000 vehicles daily resulted in a 78% reduction in fatalities and a 46% decrease in the number of crashes at access points. That is undoubtedly lifesaving, I'd say!

So how many road-marking professionals do you know and get inspiration from? Let me up that number for you.

Since its inception in 1997, STiM Group, headquartered on the border with Poland in Brest, Belarus, has reinvented itself at least fifteen times.

Starting from the development of its own road-marking equipment, the company's business model grew to include a portfolio of products (paints, thermoplastics, glass beads, and much more), services (road building, road surface marking, traffic design and optimization), and auxiliary businesses (building construction, real estate development, education). The company's "secret sauce to success" is combining diversity and focus: It started with productions of road-marking machines, then provided materials those machines needed, then developed raw materials (such as glass beads reflecting light within the road mark or resins needed for paint), then moved on to providing road construction and marking services.

As a result, the overall STiM ecosystem is as diverse as it is cost-efficient.

> " **To survive and thrive, since 1997 STiM has reinvented itself every 1.4 years.**

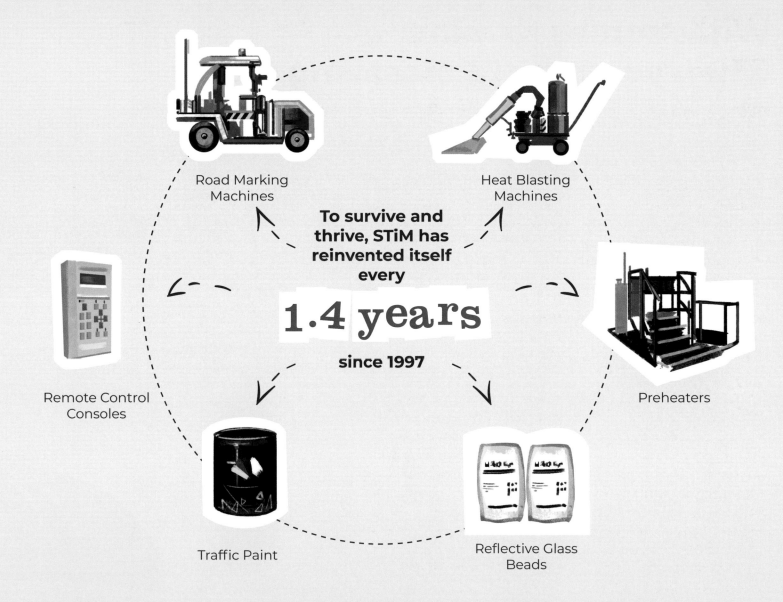

Road Marking Machines

Heat Blasting Machines

Remote Control Consoles

Preheaters

To survive and thrive, STiM has reinvented itself every

1.4 years

since 1997

Traffic Paint

Reflective Glass Beads

With this commitment to reinvention, STiM has always been more of a Titan rather than a Titanic

Business reinvention took the company to many international waters when StiM decided to diversify not only the product portfolio, but also the manufacturing locations. It built plants in Poland and Russia in addition to Belarus, all while partnering as a supplier to thirty-six countries, including Bulgaria, Romania, Germany, Italy, Finland, France, South Korea, Switzerland, the United States, and many others.

Betting on diversity and decentralization within infrastructure focus has become core to STiM's agility. When a crisis struck one region or threatened a particular product line, the group always had something else to keep it afloat. As a result, the company holds a dominating position in certain categories. For example, in road-marking materials in 2019, STiM had 70% of market share in Poland, 70% in Lithuania, 60% of in Belarus, and 45% in Russia.

Another strategic bet is the use of high tech: Much of the production is fully automated and robotized, while the products' technical performance rivals the likes of Tesla. No wonder the company's driverless (so that road workers don't get killed by reckless drivers!) laser-assisted road-marking machine Kontur 700 went viral with nearly 14 million views on the popular news platform Tech Insider.

Yet to survive the endless storm, product, process, and business model reinvention are not enough

In 2018, STiM understood that in order to thrive in the ever-increasing volatility of the global economy, it needed to radically rethink its governance, structure, and culture. For the longest time, the company's founder, Dmitry Chernenko, led every reinvention and served as the hub in the wheel that kept STiM constantly in motion. But as the company grew, decentralization of reinvention efforts was needed as well.

To start the reboot, STiM's entire twenty-two-member executive team organized an anonymous group test using the Titanic Syndrome Diagnostic tool and built an entire strategic session around the results.

The results of the diagnostic showed a respectable score in the upper 30s, which as you remember from the grading scale a few pages ago, means that the company had reasonable change and reinvention skills but a growing risk of Titanic Syndrome.

What was particularly telling and therefore valuable for the team was the breakdown of the overall score into the three categories: anticipating change, designing change, and implementing change. Out of the entire total, 15.34 points came from only one category: anticipating change.

This means that once the disruption was identified,

STiM had strong capabilities in designing the response and then executing it to results. But noticing those disruptions on time, again and again, was not the team's strongest suit.

This insight was unnoticeable to the team prior to the diagnostic, but there was a reasonable explanation. As a privately owned company ran by a strong founder, it got all its input about new threats and opportunities from a singular point, the Chief Executive Officer. Once the product portfolio, geographic presence, and production footprint grew, "keeping an ear to the ground" became an increasingly more difficult task for one person. A system had to be built.

As a result, Dmitry Chernenko stepped down as CEO and took up the role of Chairman of the Board while creating a new company in the group to run personally. It's dedicated to sensing new threats and turning them into opportunities through rapid prototyping without constant disruption or competition with the existing operations. Named STiM Labs, the new company is going deeper with "no

human needed" solutions to road marking, assuring even greater safety for road workers; developing big data solutions, providing most efficient logistics while decreasing stress on the road surface; and building a total suite of services around optimization of urban mobility.

The first tests are incredibly promising: In Belarus the overall mortality rate from mobility has gone down three times in five years, with Brest city reaching the level of one death per 100,000 inhabitants yearly, compared with five deaths per 100,000 in the neighboring European Union.

Profitability followed as from 2018 to 2019, the company profit more than doubled.

Your personal take-aways

What does the case of STiM teach you? What can you take into your personal life & career, your team, and your company?

For my life & career	For my team	For my organization

How can you turn the story of Titanic and the Titanic Syndrome test into a tool for building a common language and common action in your life and work? What can you do, from a dinner conversation with friends to a company-wide test, that can make you and your organization more resilient and disruption-ready today?

What should be done	By when	Who should be involved

We just completed the WHY portion of the book

By now, I hope I made you fall in love (OK, maybe not love, but at least strong interest) with the idea of constant change as the new normal as well as made a strong case for fundamentally rethinking and reinventing the way we do business.

Now is the time to explore how we are supposed to deal with all this chaos, volatility, uncertainty, the shortening of company and product life cycles, and the epidemic of Titanic Syndrome. What can we do to stay afloat, and how do we assure the health of our companies and our careers for today and tomorrow?

The WHAT and the HOW are where we go next. We'll build on the experience of real companies to help you reinvent your products, leadership practices, and business models to meet new market demands and prepare for incoming disruptions.

Get ready for new cases along with "how-to" canvases and tools to make your reinvention process easier and more effective.

Until then, check out additional WHY resources on the following pages: books and articles that are essential for building your reinvention toolkit.

We selected each of the books and articles for their practical value — the ability to bring immediate benefit while still going deep and thorough.

We hope that you not only will go through these resources, but also will use them as a springboard for meaningful and impactful conversations with your team, your company, and your community.

All hands on deck! It is time to get your ship ready for any storm or any iceberg.

Let's get right to it!

If you want different answers, start asking different questions.

Nadya Zhexembayeva

Building your reinvention toolkit

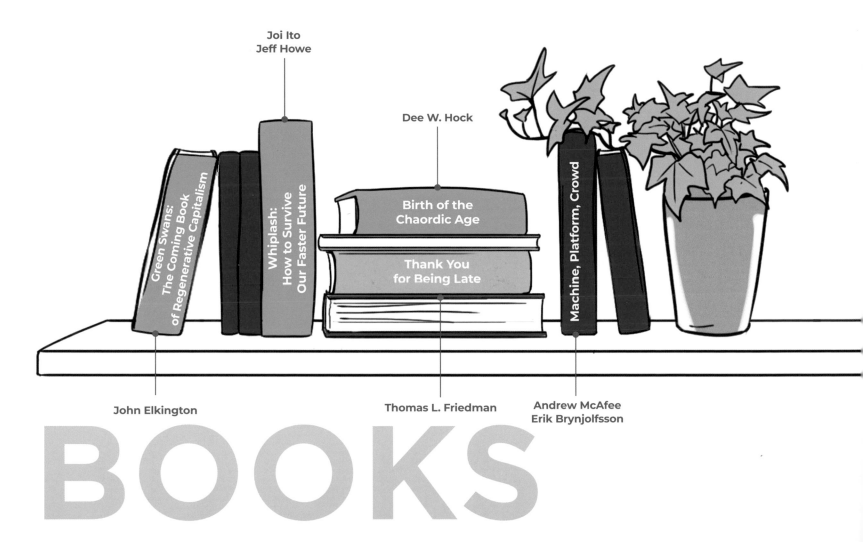

Joi Ito
Jeff Howe

Dee W. Hock

Green Swans:
The Coming Book
of Regenerative Capitalism

Whiplash:
How to Survive
Our Faster Future

Birth of the
Chaordic Age

Thank You
for Being Late

Machine, Platform, Crowd

John Elkington

Thomas L. Friedman

Andrew McAfee
Erik Brynjolfsson

BOOKS

A number of outstanding books and articles offer even more insights on *the why* of reinvention. We feature our top picks here — and you can always get links to these resources and find even more helpful tools at **www.ChiefReinventionOfficer.com/resources**

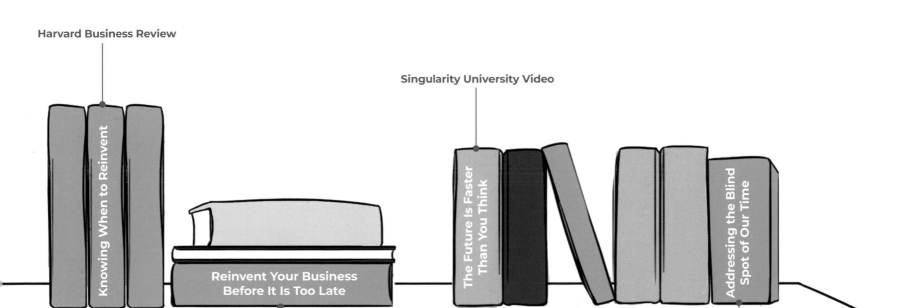

Harvard Business Review

Knowing When to Reinvent

Singularity University Video

The Future Is Faster Than You Think

Reinvent Your Business Before It Is Too Late

Addressing the Blind Spot of Our Time

Harvard Business Review

Executive Summaries by Otto Scharmer

ARTICLES

PART 2

WHAT

TO DO
TO STAY AFLOAT

THE ONLY WAY TO STAY IN BUSINESS IS TO REINVENT

We spent the first part of the book exploring why companies sink. Now that we understand the drivers and symptoms of the Titanic Syndrome, and even more importantly, the fundamental changes that make our world more turbulent and unpredictable than ever, it is time to turn to the central question.

So what?
What's the cure?
What can we do to stay afloat?

For most businesses we worked with or studied, the initial knee jerk reaction is to brace for the disaster, hold on to the past as much as possible, and pray that it all blows over.

"We just need to wait for the market to recover, and then it is business as usual!"

"The trouble with suppliers is a freak disruption, so let's just wait and see."

"It is too risky to act on incomplete information. Let's allow things to develop — we can always tighten our belts."

Sound familiar?

This desire to hold on, to cling to the past, to endure whatever the harsh environment has to offer, is well documented by social scientists. A 2010 study, for example, found that the longer something is thought to exist, the better it is evaluated, whether we talk about university requirements, art, acupuncture, or food.

Dr. Heidi Grant Halvorson writes: "People who saw a painting described as having been painted in 1905 found it far more pleasing to look at than people who saw the same painting described as created in 2005.

"Students preferred the course requirement described as the status quo over a new version regardless of whether the new version meant more or less coursework.

"People who were told that acupuncture had been in existence for 2,000 years expressed more favorable attitudes toward it than those who were told it existed for 250 years.

"Study participants were given a piece of European chocolate. It was described to them as having first been sold in its region either seventy-three years ago or three years ago. Guess which group rated the chocolate as better-tasting...?"

We really like to keep things around for as long as possible. Neuroscience of leadership shows that our brain requires much more energy to deal with new choices than to revert to old routines – and thus tries to avoid it. We also tend to see new things as a potential threat, evoking the fight-or-flight response that takes over our body in an attempt to protect ourselves against a real or imaginary enemy. It's no won-

der that we see change as a negative. In organizations, that shows up as outright resistance to change. 2005 research, for example, suggested that of all the emotions we feel toward change, three primary ones are cynicism, fear, and acceptance. Two of these emotions are fiercely negative and one vaguely positive. Intensely positive emotions never made the top of the list. For anyone who survived organizational transformation, this negative bias is hardly surprising.

The desire to hang onto things as long as possible and avoid change at all costs drives us to create endless lockdown rules and excessive regulations, to design rigid processes and detailed instructions, and to celebrate

books that showcase businesses that are "built to last" (which happens to be the title of an exceptionally good book!).

We all want to last.

To continue.

To get back to "business as usual."

We want to hold on to the world just the way it is.

And that is where the central problem lies — and why so many business transformation efforts are doomed. It is the desire to stick with, to sustain no matter what, that ultimately gets us killed.

Why?

Sustainability doesn't drive life. Change does.

Every second of every day, things change, even us. We breathe in and out, becoming a different person with every molecule of oxygen that enters our bloodstream. (Incidentally, did you know that every single day you are guaranteed to inhale at least one of the molecules of air that passed through Genghis Khan's lungs?)

We see the seasons turn on the calendar and eat foods produced through the gradual change called growth.

We survive the ups and downs of the stock exchange and come in and out of economic recessions.

Remember the statistics from Part One? If we counted only country-level recessions and forgot about industry or global recessions, that still would mean an average of one recession every twenty-five days!

Nothing in the world holds on.

So if holding on or locking down don't work, what can we do? How do companies survive? How can we sustain?

It will sound almost paradoxical.

The secret of true sustainability is simple: Take the essence of what you are and let go of everything else. That essential core is what you need to propel forward, reinventing

yourself vigorously over and over again, with staggering rapidity.

The secret is reinvention.

Let's dive in.

WHAT IS REINVENTION?

For a section that starts with such a demanding question, you might expect a clear and immediate answer. We'll get to the definition soon, I promise, but first, allow me to take you on a journey.

We started this journey in Part One with a look at the rapidly changing context for our lives and work. In 2018, out of more than 2,000 participants in our Global Reinvention Survey, 47% reported that in order to survive and thrive, they needed to reinvent their businesses every three years or less. In 2020, that number jumped to 58%.

This need to reinvent more often should come as no shock, given the deep interconnections and interdependence that come with participating in a global economy. The World Economic Forum's *2019 Global Risk Report* mapped out thirty critical risks across five categories — economic, environmental, geopolitical, societal, and technological — and showed the connections among them. The spread of infectious disease was one of the top ten. COVID-19 (or something like it) was fully anticipated, and many other projected disruptions probably will emerge and force change in our lives, organizations, and communities.

Turbulence is here to stay. The year 2020 is when the International Monetary Fund celebrated the sixtieth anniversary of its annual World Uncertainty Index, and it showed the highest levels of uncertainty we've experienced. In these decades, we've seen many ups and downs, including assassinations of world leaders, oil embargos, and military crises, but today our world is significantly more unpredictable than ever before.

Aside from risks, many other factors are disrupting and rearranging the ways we live and work. New technology,

new competition, new regulations, new generations (think Millennials, Generation Z, and beyond) all drive new expectations for our products, services, and society at large.

Whether we like it or not, we don't seem to have a choice. In the coming years, our lives and our businesses will face more disruption than ever before. The only choice we have is this: Either we'll fight change, seeing it as our enemy in a desperate attempt to hold on to our past, or we'll use change, turning it to our competitive advantage.

The trouble is that although we recognize and even anticipate the risks and opportunities that change brings, we are not good at adapting to them. We have developed a wide range of theories and approaches to help us succeed — strategy, foresight, design thinking, continuous improvement, agile, scrum, innovation, organizational development, and

change management, to name a few — and the numbers are not showing progress. Two decades ago, in a 2000 Harvard Business Review article, Nitin Nohria and Michael Beer observed that "about 70% of all change initiatives fail." Today, according to global consulting firm BCG, we've gotten worse at it: "75% of transformation efforts don't deliver the hoped-for results."

> **The trouble is that although we recognize and even anticipate the risks and opportunities that change brings, we are not good at adapting to them.**

It's a small wonder that companies seem to stay successful for shorter spans. The 2018 Corporate Longevity Forecast conducted by Innosight showed that in 1964, S&P 500 companies would stay on the list for an average of thirty-three years. It "narrowed to twenty-four years by 2016 and is forecast to shrink to just twelve years by 2027."

This suggests that there's something profoundly wrong with our basic assumptions about how change works. Reinvention is a way to remedy these wrongs and invite crucial shifts in the way we think about, design, and implement change. Often, these are based on a perspective that is opposite to what you may have believed in the past.

We call these "flips," and there are five that every reinventor must consider. We'll look first at each flip theoretically, then turn to practical cases from different countries and industries to illustrate how everything comes together.

> **75% of transformation efforts don't deliver the hoped-for results. This suggests that there's something profoundly wrong with our basic assumptions about how change works.**

Flip #1

From: Change happens rarely

To: Change is a constant

Modern management was born during times of relative stability, as almost every prominent business solution emerged in the West after World War II. This includes the book many treat as "the birth of modern business thinking": the 1946 *Concept of the Corporation* by the legendary Peter Drucker.

Of course, some isolated wars and disruptions continued, but in the second part of the twentieth century, the Western world seemed to stabilize: no significant global conflict, relatively stable borders, and no fundamental economic disruptions. Most manage-ment functions, such as strategy, human resources, operations research, innovation, and IT (information technology), were professionalized in this postwar era of relative stability. And many of our most beloved management tools and frameworks, such as Just-in-Time production, TQM (total quality management), and even fixed budgets were developed for a business environment that was relatively predictable.

As I mentioned in this handbook's introduction, for many years, the data seemed to justify the assumption of stability built into our business operating systems.

Stéphane Garelli, a world authority on competitiveness and a Professor Emeritus at IMD where he founded the World Competitiveness Cen-tre, spoke of our no-longer-stable world this way: "You will probably live longer than most big companies. The large companies of today are not the same as the ones of yesterday. The process of creative destruction highlighted by Schumpeter is still in action. Indeed, it is accelerating. A recent study by McKinsey found that the average life-span of companies listed in Standard & Poor's 500 was 61 years in 1958. Today, it is less than 18 years. McKinsey believes that, in 2027, 75% of the companies currently quoted on the S&P 500 will have disappeared."

Corporations worldwide enjoyed long and healthy lives, with a slow rise to the top of financial performance and a gradual decline to annihilation. The rate of change was so slow, and crises were so rare that reinvention was rarely needed — and when it was, we had all the time in the world to renew our business on our terms, a once-in-a-lifetime project.

But the predictable postwar world, if it ever existed, is long gone.

Judging by the evidence, the acceleration picked up in the late 1980s and early 1990s, whereby globalization — think the fall of the Berlin Wall, the collapse of the Soviet Union and the socialist bloc, the opening of China — mixed with the Internet and the-dot.com boom. In the same period, the population grew by nearly 70%. Ideas, capital, products, connections, and knowledge became more accessible to more people – and started moving among them with more ease and higher speed.

By the early 2000s, the concept of VUCA – the four world conditions of volatility, uncertainty, complexity, and ambiguity – turned up in management books, such as the 2007 *Get There Early: Sensing the Future to Compete in the Present* by Bob Johansen. And by the 2020s, we approached a point where many forces — social, economic, political, and technological — are coming together in a whole new way.

Singularity University co-founder Peter Diamandis and his co-authors of the 2020 book *The Future Is Faster Than You Think* speak of this new moment of our history as a convergence point, where "AI, robotics, virtual reality, digital biology, and sensors crash into 3D printing, blockchain, quantum computing, and global gigabit networks... We

have now found clear evidence to believe that the rate at which technology is accelerating is itself accelerating."

Companies are expected to reinvent themselves and their products faster than ever before. However, to do so, we first must flip the fundamental beliefs that drive our management systems.

Psychologists define a mindset as a combination of beliefs and deep-rooted thoughts. Studies after studies show that what we believe changes how we act and what we achieve. Take Carol Dweck and her research on fixed versus growth mindset as a great deep dive of how mindsets work.

Our thoughts literally create our reality. And before I lose all my academic and data-loving-businesswoman credibility, let me explain what I mean.

Our thoughts, the fundamental beliefs we have about something, define how we behave, make decisions, and allocate resources.

If you think that change happens rarely, you will act far differently than if you think that change is a regular event — just as if you think that snow falls only every fifty years, you will act far differently than if you think it comes every winter.

If snow (and change!) happens rarely, there is no need to prepare, to allocate resources, or to develop skills for dealing with it.

If snow (and change!) happens regularly, it's time to invest in winter tires, to prepare the city infrastructure, and to consider how to turn snow into a resource, an opportunity, or an advantage.

So to survive and thrive in our turbulent times, the first flip we need to make is to stop treating change as an exception to a rule and to start seeing it as a normal part of our daily life. As one coder told me in a funky software development language, change is a feature, not a bug.

Want an example of this and other flips in action?
Turn to page 96!

Here is a quick exercise to get this flip going: Explore what kinds of management solutions are needed for a long company life cycle (let's take an average of seventy-five years) and what kinds of approaches are needed for a short cycle (let's assume an average of seven years).

75 _____

7 _____

What kind of skills and capabilities are needed to succeed?

What's the safest way to approach your product portfolio?

What is the best way to approach financial planning? What's the optimal level of debt? How should you budget?

Flip #2

From: **If it ain't broke, don't fix it**

To: **Break it before somebody else does**

Many axioms drive our personal and organizational life. Along with "We've always done it this way," "Don't fix it if it ain't broken" has long been a beacon of truth to follow.

This approach might be helpful during slow and steady times, but when we enter the era of chaos, turbulence, and constant disruption, it becomes nearly deadly. Consultants Paul Nunes and Tim Breene explain it perfectly: "Sooner or later, all businesses, even the most successful, run out of room to grow.

Faced with this unpleasant reality, they are compelled to reinvent themselves periodically. The ability to pull off this difficult feat — to jump from the maturity stage of one business to the growth stage of the next — is what separates high performers from those whose time at the top is all too brief."

The potential consequences are dire for any organization that fails to reinvent itself in time. As Matthew S. Olson and Derek van Bever demonstrate in their book *Stall Points,* once a company runs into a major stall in its growth, it has less than a 10% chance of fully recovering. Those odds are certainly daunting, and they do much to explain why two-thirds of stalled companies are later acquired, taken private, or forced into bankruptcy.

In other words, if we start reinventing on a decline, on the red side of our company life cycle, the chances that we'll be able to restore our company to its peak performance are only 10%. If we start fixing things when they appear to be broken, it is a 90% probability that we are doomed.

To reinvent successfully, we must forget "If it's not broken, don't fix it." It's time to break our organization, our products, and our processes before somebody else does and to build a new one with our employees fully engaged.

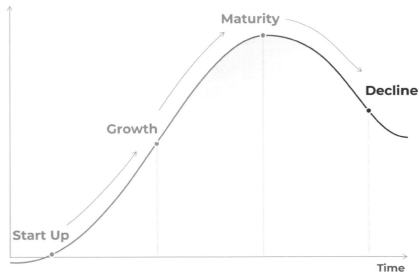

Flip #3

From: Run a spo-radic project in reaction to change

To: Build a deli-berate system for proactive reinvention

Since "Change is not a project" is the title of this book's introduction, I will not spend much time rehashing the same data and argument. But this particular flip comes logically as a continuation of the previous one: When change comes often, the most efficient and effective way to manage it is to be systematic, deliberate, and proactive.

When change was rare, it was OK to treat it as a rare project, an occasional fire to put out, or an opportunity to catch. You also didn't need to develop your own capacity for reinvention because it could be outsourced to consultants and specialists.

But once change becomes the norm, it's time to build a system, a method, or a process and strengthen your reinvention muscles to make that system work for you. That way, you can prevent most fires and tackle the ones that could not be prevented with greater focus, proficiency, and ease.

Flip #4

From: Bet on the new

To: Preserve the best of the old while fostering the new

Resistance to change has long been cited as one of the key reasons why companies fail to adapt on time. As I show in my 2020 Harvard Business Review article, research confirms how few employees are ready to take the risks needed to reinvent. A team at the University of Toronto surveyed 1,000 American and Canadian knowledge workers (all employed and with college degrees) to assess qualities such as "grit" and "openness to risk" across two countries and three age groups (younger than 35, 35 to 44, and older than 45). While the drive for innovation among participants varied from 14% to 28%, only two of the six different groups measured broke the 25% mark. Willingness to take a risk was even more telling: At best, 19% of your company is willing, with some age groups dipping as low as 11%.

I first discovered this dirty little secret shortly after leaving my safe job as a business school professor to start my own consulting business, focusing on (you guessed it) helping companies learn how to change.

Here I was, armed with the latest research, fired up with ideas to help my client, a global mining company, become more agile and responsive to change, only to find myself in the middle of a processing facility face to face with a line manager bluntly asking me: "Are you smoking something at your board meetings!?"

Since then, I've heard this question posed in various ways at some point in every single project on which I've worked. Only a few weeks ago, at the annual strategic session of a global consumer goods company, I was told point-blank: "For you people, innovation is all that. For us, it's extra work with no results or — much worse — lost jobs."

I understand the source of this frustration. Often business transformation projects get cooked up behind closed doors by a small group of economists and consultants detached from the reality on the ground. Moving a few numbers in a spreadsheet seems objective and rational until you understand that there are legacies, jobs, and lives involved.

To counter this ever-present resistance, it's crucial to find a balance between preserving the old and fostering the new. That way you connect the past, the present, and the future, bringing the resistance down and driving engagement up.

Want an example of this and other flips in action? Turn to page 96!

Flip #5

From: Fix the problem we have today

To: Succeed today while building up tomorrow

For decades, much of the world developed an unhealthy love affair with quick fixes. Have a headache? Take a pill. Need to lose weight? Go for liposuction. Facing a shortage of cash? Lay off some "headcount." (Yes, we don't even want to call people *people*.)

When it comes to our approach to business investing and decision-making, hyper-focus on everything quick and short term is particularly noticeable. As economic correspondent Alana Semu-els shows, "The average holding time for stocks has fallen from eight years in 1960 to eight months in 2016. Almost 80 percent of chief financial officers at 400 of America's largest public companies say they would sacrifice a firm's economic value to meet the quarter's earnings expectations." That is scary data!

Saving today at the expense of tomorrow has become a norm. Equally dangerous is excessive focus on the future without a grounding in the present. As a recovering academic, I made this mistake so many times: building a vision of a rosy future without investing time and effort to figure out the pragmatic bridges between that distant future and the very different, complex, and messy present.

How do we not only avoid Titanic Syndrome but also prevent endless firefighting or blind idealism?

Professionals and companies that manage to navigate the chaos do both: succeeding today while building a foundation for tomorrow. That's the true purpose and measure of successful reinvention.

> **For decades, much of the world developed an unhealthy love affair with quick fixes. Saving today at the expense of tomorrow has become a norm.**

Take all five flips together...

...And you arrive at a new definition of what reinvention is and what it's not. Reinvention is the cure to the plight of Titanic Syndrome and a way to find a win for today as well as tomorrow. It is not about a short-term win or long-term wishful thinking. Rather, it is a balance between reflection and action that is deliberate, proactive, and systematic.

Reinvention is a reflection of a mindset shift in a way we see and succeed at change – similar to how a shift from fixed to growth mindset changes our learning outcomes. Throughout the years, our global community of reinventors has come up with different definitions of reinvention that highlight a different angle or dimension of this way of thinking and working:

- Reinvention is a practice of **embracing** change by **re-imagining** and **remaking** something so that it manifests new and improved attributes, qualities, and results.

- It is a **systematic** approach to thriving in chaos that includes ongoing anticipation, design, and implementation of change **via continuous sense-making, anticipatory and emergent learning,** and **synthesis** of cross-boundary, cross-disciplinary, and cross-functional knowledge.

- It's a way to foster sustainability of a system by **dynamically harmonizing** continuity and change.

- Reinvention is an **immune system** designed to ensure systematic health for individuals and organizations.

- And, perhaps, for my fellow pragmatists, the most actionable definition: Reinvention is a systematic approach of engaging in **healthy cycles of planned renewal,** building on the past to ensure current and future viability.

To capture the true essence and the core purpose of re-invention, I have put together a framework that speaks of the three dangerous traps that leaders and organizations fall into — and the one true "North Star" of reinvention, which aims to assure a successful today and a thriving tomorrow. After months of testing and improving, our global community of reinventors has affectionately called it the TOTO Matrix (which is the shorter version of the original tool title, "Today-To-morrow Matrix").

To survive and thrive in a risky, interconnected world of constant flux, you must make re-invention a part of daily life. This is not a project you do once, like building a forever home. It's much more like being a child who's growing up all the time: Your body and the way your brain works change with every year that passes.

And in my book (pun intended!), staying in the perpetual state of childlike openness, growth, and renewal sounds exactly like what we need right now.

Are you ready to reinvent?

> **To survive and thrive in a risky, interconnected world of constant flux, you must make reinvention a part of daily life.**

Winning today and tomorrow with the TOTO Matrix

Succeeding Today

+/-

FIREFIGHTING
Short-term fix, long-term pain

1. Reactive and defensive response to change that leads to chronic exhaustion
2. One-off unsystematic efforts with little-to-no alignment: love for shiny objects, hot topics, and burning platforms
3. Bias against anticipation & reflection

+/+

REINVENTION
Solving today while building up tomorrow

1. Proactive, deliberate, and embracing approach to change
2. Balanced practical action to preserve the best of the old while fostering the new
3. Focus on building a system for timely reinvention

Jeopardizing Tomorrow

Thriving Tomorrow

TITANIC SYNDROME
We only see the disaster when it hits us

1. Arrogance or overconfidence: "Too big or too good to fail"
2. Trust in past success "We've always done it this way"
3. Inability to anticipate and adapt to change

-/-

BLIND IDEALISM
Wishing for tomorrow while destroying today

1. Disconnected from present reality and pressing needs
2. Wishful thinking
3. Bias against implementation: heavy focus on strategy, often impractical and untested

-/+

Failing Today

Reinvention
A DEEP DIVE

Now that we've covered the essential nature of reinvention — the creative act of balancing the needs of the present and the hopes of the future — it's time to take a deep dive into making all of this theory work for you.

To do that, we'll look at three different stories of reinvention: a manufacturing company in Slovenia, a cosmetics company in the United Kingdom, and a service business in the United States. Like the very first reinvention case we shared in Part 1, these too will end with practical exercises to warm up your transformation muscles.

Then we'll provide you with a map, or even better, a radar to find your next direction in reinvention and offer a powerful tool for reinventing your business model. After that, it's all about you doing the work: Reinvention is not a spectator sport.

The task in front of you is simple but not easy. (*Simple* and *easy* are two very different things). Instead of desperately trying to stay in business by all means possible, it is time for you to get out of that business and into a new one.

To get you going, we are building a collection of cases with fresh ideas and hands-

on exercises that will help you answer the key question: What should I reinvent in my business?

These cases will give insights into the wide variety you have to choose from, and later we'll offer even more examples to inspire you.

case #2
HIDRIA

A company with a rich past, Hidria found itself in search of new history. Located in a tiny mining town, the business of producing air-conditioning products was being squeezed. squeezed: on one side by increasing competition from top-priced Western brands and on the other by cheap Chinese imports. How can Hidria survive — or even thrive?

case #3
LUSH

While the traditional majority of cosmetic companies are fighting for a share of the difficult consumer market with more appealing packaging and stronger advertising campaigns, and while the eco-conscious minority is struggling with recycled plastic and third-party «green» certification, Lush goes well below the surface and delivers an entirely new way of looking at a product.

case #4
PENZONE

It is February 2019, and a week ago this salon brought home the coveted title of Salon of the Year at the North American Hairstyling Awards, held in California. Yet it is snowing outside, and Dublin, Ohio is a far cry from the limelight of Hollywood. What is even more remarkable is that the PENZONE isn't a newcomer: This innovative, award-winning, homegrown brand is fifty years old. How did a small hair salon survive and thrive while the giants disappeared?

HIDRIA

From air conditioning to electric cars? Why not!

It happens to me with a surprising frequency. A short email, a quick phone call, a Facebook post, and suddenly you feel as if all's right with the world. Like there is true justice. Like good guys do finish first. This was one of those emails.

Brief and to the point, professional as ever, Iztok Seljak, president of the Management Board of Hidria, shared the happy news: beating more than 15,000 other companies, Hidria won the title of Europe's most innovative company of the year. That put a smile on my face!

Over the past decade, Seljak, a fearless leader, an inspiring colleague, and a frequent speaker at my executive MBA classes, has championed his team to invent its way out of disappearance. A company with a rich past, by the early 2000s Hidria found itself in search of new history. Located in the tiny mining town of Idrija in western Slovenia, in a beautiful valley surrounded by Alpine mountains, Hidria's business of producing air-conditioning products was being squeezed: on one side by increasing competition from top-priced Western brands and on the other by cheap Chinese imports. What most companies do in this situation is cut costs, lay people off, tighten the belt, and weather the storm. But Hidria decided to follow a different path. With its core competence in producing electric motors for cooling and heating systems, the question was: Is there anywhere else this skill might be useful? It turned out there was, indeed.

> **❝ What most companies do in this situation is cut costs, lay people off, tighten the belt, and weather the storm. But Hidria decided to follow a different path.**

With the turn of the century, the pressure to reduce harmful emissions, coupled with the rapid growth in fuel prices and the development of battery technology and infrastructure, finally turned an electric motor into a legitimate new business idea. While fuel cell and other technologies are still far from mass commercialization, the introduction of electric motors for hybrid or pure electric vehicles was the easiest way to meet the demands of the new legislation. The problem was that few automotive powerhouses in the world had a strong competence in building an electric motor, and even fewer automotive suppliers had innovated in this domain. But a company producing electric motors for air conditioning and heating systems did.

The entire Executive MBA class chuckles as Seljak reflects. But that is where the secret of Hidria's success lies: the ability to constantly look at the business anew. They call it "embedded business model innovation."

" Why did we enter electric mobility? We were young, full of new ideas, and hungry to go beyond following to leading. When we started, the entire automotive industry had already proclaimed this domain of innovation as a worthless, short-lived fad non-deserving of any significant attention. Thankfully, we did not know that at the time.

Value creation, reimagined

In 2004, Hidria turned its business on its head by adding ecologically green mobility to its mission, vision, and core strategy. In 2005, its first year of operations, the new automotive division brought in revenues of €10 million (about $13 million U.S.). By 2012, amid the global economic recession, Hidria reached the profitable automotive revenues of €150 million (nearly $200 million U.S.).

In 2016, the Hidria Optymus PSG engine cold-start system was given an award for Green Innovation of the Year. In the next two years, Hidria won the Best Supplier Award from PSA Peugeot Citroen Opel.

Today, esteemed top-of-the-line models produced by Audi, BMW, Mercedes-Benz, Porsche, Ford, Opel, Citroen, Peugeot, Renault, and Volkswagen, among others, all rely on Hidria's products:

- The engine of **every fifth** new diesel-powered car globally is ignited by Hidria's **ignition solutions.**

- **Every fifth** new car in Europe is steered by Hidria's **electrical power-steering** solutions.

- Every third new car in Europe is powered by Hidria's **hybrid and electrical power-train** solutions.

There is no question that everyone likes this kind of Cinderella story: from nothing to top of the world in a few easy steps. The most interesting question is: How did Hidria get there?

Seljak explains, "They all think that it is all about technological innovation. That, of course, is important. But it is not what truly makes the difference. Time and again, our victories depend on the ability to imagine an entirely new way of adding value. That is what business model innovation is about: value creation, reimagined. Continuously."

+$200 m

amidst global recession

Harnessing the power of horizontal breakthroughs

Hidria's embedded business-model innovation is not contained within a particular product line or division. All divisions of the company got on board with thinking differently and imagining an entirely new set of solutions for a resource-deprived world.

With three new research-and-development institutes, each stocked with a range of laboratories, the company continues pushing the development of comprehensive, financially viable mobility and indoor air services. Turning solar power into a cooling/air-conditioning system instead of a heating/electricity system is a technical innovation; figuring out how to make it work financially as a viable product is a business-model innovation.

Often, Hidria alone cannot achieve such innovation, so the company uses a number of "co-opetition" projects, collaborating with its competitors for whole-system breakthroughs.

In 2011, together with seven of its competitors and the Slovenian government, Hidria became a founding partner of a new for-profit private-public partnership, SiEVA, focused on co-development of technological solutions for ecologically clean cars.

In 2012, the company initiated a new sustainable-construction consortium, putting its climate-control solutions to good use. Uniting more than forty companies across Europe, the award-winning Feniks consortium brought

2011

2012

together a workforce of 35,000 people with annual revenue of €4.5 billion (at that time, around $6 billion U.S.). Building for the Sochi 2014 Olympics was among the first big victories for the consortium.

In 2019, Hidria initiated the €8 billion (around $9 billion U.S.) EDISON WINCI consortium, turning its attention to the infrastructure and logistical systems for contactless charging of electric vehicles.

Also in 2019, it united with eleven leading European institutions (research organ-izations as well as production companies, including Volkswagen) to establish Project SOPHIA for the creation of a new generation of core robotic technologies for socially cooperative human-robot systems.

From air conditioning to electric car motors, to construction, to infrastructure, and finally to robotics. Continuously reimagining value creation, exploring fresh angles, and embracing diverse partnerships. That's Hidria.

And that is what inventing-new business models looks like. United we stand!

> **Often, Hidria alone cannot achieve such innovation, so the company uses a number of "co-opetition" projects, collaborating with its competitors for whole-system breakthroughs.**

Now

2019

Your personal take-aways

Think of your strengths (assets, resources, competences) and how can you apply them in a fresh way (for new products or services, in other industries, regions, for different customer segments, etc.)

Strengths: Current assets, resources, competences	Fresh use

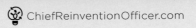

What collaborations do you currently have, and what new partnerships can you explore?

<table>
<tr><td>Current collaborations
and partnerships</td><td>Possible new (even unlikely)
collaborations to explore</td></tr>
</table>

LUSH

It is green, dense, and surprisingly light

Fitting perfectly in the palm of your hand, it leaves a light, oily residue on your skin. It is fragrant (just a touch of soft, alluring smell) and textured (like thousands of little worms squished together). It goes against everything we were taught by conventional strategy theory.

And it is an amazingly powerful symbol of the new era dawning.

So what is it? Let's take a close look.

A soap bar?

A spinach hamburger?

A sponge?

A sort of energy tablet?

An eco-macaroon?

A new-age vitamin pill?

A breakthrough detergent?

In front of you is the equivalent of not one, not two, but three bottles of shampoo — all squished into one solid bar.

That's the way to reinvent!

Now think about it.
What do we sell when we sell shampoo?

What end benefit do the customers get? What is the value? Clean hair, indeed. What ingredient doesn't need to be supplied at the time of the sale to ensure this desired outcome, as it is always available to the customer at home? Water, indeed. So why do we pump water, process water, bottle water, package water, store water, transport water, sell water, and waste plastic post-water just to wash our hair, when water is the only ingredient that we don't need to provide?

That was the starting point for Lush Fresh Handmade Cosmetics, a twenty-year-old UK brand, when it started working on reinventing the traditional shampoo. According to the company, "The inventors worked with Stan Krysztal" — one of the leading cosmetic chemists of Great Britain — "to create these very clever little bars; an effective, hardworking shampoo base with quality ingredients, beautiful fragrances, and, best of all, they require no packaging. Handy for traveling, compact, and easy to use, each bar is roughly the equivalent of three plastic bottles of shampoo. These humble bars are (probably) one of the greatest inventions we've ever come up with."

The Lush team loves talking about it. But what about the customers? Naturally, some customers would refuse such a strange-looking shampoo option. My baby brother is one of them. Whenever he visits us, I have to make a conscious effort to restock his bathroom. "I am a normal person," he claims. "I like my soap solid and my shampoo liquid, and not the other way around!"

Yet by any measure other than my brother's comfort zone, Lush's solid invention has been a great success since its launch in 2007, capturing rave reviews and a solid (pun intended!) customer following. Here is one of such reviews from a rather conventional consumer — a *Boston.com* writer's take:

" Trust me, I was skeptical, too. A rock of shampoo, eh? Sounds about as effective as a steel wool pad as a conditioner. But after trying it multiple times at an adult sleepover — don't judge — I slowly became convinced. The stone of shampoo seems to last forever (if you keep it in a dry place after use), and it comes in a variety of scents. I recently picked up cinnamon and clove. But most important, it's pretty damn effective. The shampoo itself lathers nicely, (sorry to sound like a Prell commercial. ... Wait, do they still make that?) and at about $10 a rock, it's a better deal than it appears.

The reinvention of LUSH shampoo

BEFORE

$13.95

≈ 20 washes

Plastic, labor, and energy waste:

Producing, bottling and distributing 6+ million plastic bottles globally per year

Water waste:

At least 120, 000 gallons (or 450, 000 liters) globally per year

AFTER

$10.95

≈ 80 washes

Plastic, labor and energy savings:

2.6 ounces (or 75 grams) of plastic per shampoo bar saved

Transportation cost savings:

15 times less per wash

The glowing reviews and growing revenues are not the only business victories for Lush solid shampoo. On the other side of the business continuum, the company is doing well with its costs. As of 2019, Lush has avoided producing, bottling, and distributing 30 million plastic bottles globally in five years by selling shampoo bars — count in 2.6 ounces (or 75 grams) of plastic saved per shampoo bar, and multiply that by all the savings in energy and labor costs that would have been incurred designing, producing, bottling, and storing the bottles.

Annual water savings from producing the solid shampoos are at least 120,000 gallons (or 450,000 liters) globally. Transportation savings are beyond surprising: When calculated per wash, transportation costs are 15 times less than those of liquid shampoo. Additional resource intelligence comes in a form of

raw-material savings: The bar has no preservatives, as there is no liquid content requiring preservation. And with a scale of 930+ stores in forty-nine countries carrying the product, strengthened revenues and intelligent cost structure for the unusual product are a welcome performance outcome for the once-tiny underdog of the cosmetic industry.

No wonder a 2018 *Elle* article declared that Lush solid shampoo is "Plastic-Free Beauty Product You Need To Buy ASAP!"

30 000 000 plastic bottles

15 times less transportation costs

120 000 gallons of water

Lush solid shampoo is a story of true reinvention

While the traditional majority of cosmetic companies are fighting for a share of the difficult consumer market with more appealing packaging and stronger advertising campaigns, and while the eco-conscious minority is struggling with recycled plastic and third-party «green» certification, Lush goes well below the surface and delivers an entirely new way of looking at a product.

Once a barely known company that started with a sausage machine in a messy workshop of a nearly bankrupt husband-and-wife team, Lush has put into question the essential value delivered by traditional shampoos and paved the way for an entirely new

way of thinking. Lush's solid-shampoo bar exemplifies the company's production standards. About 70% of the products sold require no packaging, much of the product range has no synthetic raw materials, and more than 70% of the range is totally unpreserved.

For Lush, reinvention is simply business as usual. For most of us, it is anything but.

Time to change?

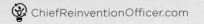
Your personal take-aways

What allowed Lush to successfully reinvent its existing product, liquid shampoo, into a better version of itself is a deep understanding of the value its current product offers.

What elements of the existing product/service are unnecessary for the customer and therefore can be removed? What elements can be added or changed?

CAN BE REMOVED

CAN BE ADDED OR CHANGED

PENZONE

The coffee is fresh and robust, with a rich foam that rivals any brew from Starbucks. Yet I'm not in a coffee shop.

The makeup counters are crowded with customers, testing the latest eyebrow trends. Yet I'm miles from the nearest Sephora.

A staffer hurries past me with a pot of warm Ayurveda oil. Yet I'm not in an alternative medicine clinic.

Where am I? At one of the many locations of PENZONE Salons+Spas.

It is February 2019, and a week ago this salon brought home the coveted title of Salon of the Year at the North American Hairstyling Awards, held in California. Yet it is snowing outside, and Dublin, Ohio, is a far cry from the limelight of Hollywood.

What is even more remarkable is that the PENZONE isn't a newcomer, unburdened by the weight of the past. This innovative, award-winning, homegrown brand is fifty years old.

At the time of its founding in 1969, PENZONE was a contemporary to some of corporate America's most powerful titans.

Take, for example, RCA. In the year of PENZONE's incorporation, RCA appeared on the Fortune 500 list as №20. A giant in electronics, radio equipment, marine, and international communications, and broadcasting. When General Electric acquired RCA in 1986, most of its assets were liquidated.

The year 1969 was also great at Pan American World Airways, known to most as Pan Am. Advertised with the slogan "The World's Most Experienced Airline," Pan Am had 150 jets flying to 86 countries on every continent except Antarctica. It made enough profit to stock up cash reserves of $1 billion.

By the late 1980s, however, the company was hit by a series of external disruptions (read: icebergs!), including rising fuel prices caused by the Gulf War. By January 1991, Pan Am filed for bankruptcy, and it closed up shop in December that year.

PENZONE, though, is still here.

How did a small hair salon from sparsely populated mid-Ohio survive and thrive while the giants disappeared?

And how does the same brand continue to grow and grab awards as a disruptor and innovator today?

Created as a single salon by Charles A. Penzone, the company was built on the idea of constant disruption. Debbie Penzone, the company's current CEO, says:

"Reinvention has been in our DNA since the beginning. Charles Penzone, our founder, loves change, and he loves inspiring others to be bold. He doesn't want to be that old leather chair that's so worn nobody sits in it."

As far back as the early 1970s, the company did the unusual. For instance, Charles brought the then-unheard-of hairstyling techniques of Vidal Sassoon to the Columbus neighborhoods, which allowed the company to grow to nine salons and 150 employees.

The year 1991 marked the company's new reinvention cycle. At that time, the country-wide average size for salons was 3,000 square feet. PENZONE went in a different direction. It built its first Grand Salon — a whopping 18,000 square feet — as a three-floor structure, consisting of hairstyling stations, manicure room, treatment rooms, an employee training area, and a private garden.

A significant boost in revenue and national press followed:

Think *Today Show, Inside Edition, Redbook, InStyle,* and *People.*

18 000
square feet

During the following decades, PENZONE opened two additional Grands while branching into new businesses and concepts.

In 1996, the company introduced an urban hair salon concept under the brand of MAX THE SALON, growing it into a healthy chain in the early 2000s. Then it added the Royal Rhino Club Barbershop & Lounge and the LIT Life + Yoga studio, adding diversity to the services and the guests PENZONE served.

Debbie Penzone illustrates:

"We tried many things. We owned a distribution company for the beauty industry, which we later sold. We even had a landscaping business! Is it scary? Yes, absolutely. But you must continue to do it, afraid. You are always going to be afraid. Do it anyway."

In 2018, the company started yet another massive reinvention cycle: rethinking its main stake business. Everything from core services to processes to branding was rethought, renewed, and reimagined.

> **Is it scary? Yes, absolutely. Do it anyway.**

BEFORE

Designed as a stand-alone building, the original Grand Salon projected a sense of classic beauty, high price, and exclusivity.

Most appointments were booked by phone.

Upon arrival, check-in counters and a waiting room took center stage.

The message to customers, whom the company sees as guests, was crystal clear: The only service you can have done right now is what you booked previously.

Any other services are by appointment only.

AFTER

The new salon concept is built with a sense of modern lines, freshness, and openness.

Appointments can be booked by phone, on the website, or through a newly minted app.

Check-in counters are surrounded by product shelves — where guests are testing new products and exchanging advice.

A bar welcomes you with teasing aromas — a centerpiece of the Social Room, which features coffee, tea, organic juices, wine, plant-based foods, and community programming.

The message to guests is clear: You're here to explore, discover, connect, and share. This is a salon, a beauty store, a coffee shop, and a community space wrapped in one. A world of possibilities awaits.

BEFORE

The space is designed for an individual customer having an individual experience.

The waiting room seats are isolated and spaced out to keep each customer to him or herself.

This room is for waiting.

The center of the brand is the founder's name.

AFTER

The space is designed to foster community and connection.

The seats are arranged around tables, fostering an easy exchange of conversation and ideas.

A coffee bar serving high-end coffee allows for a relaxed and approachable atmosphere.

This room is for connection and conversation.

The founder, Charles Penzone, accepted the team's daring proposal to rebrand by dropping his first name. Now it still honors this amazing person — but at the same time, it celebrates the entire PENZONE community and the experience that unites them.

As the first two locations were reimagined with the new PENZONE concept, the company courageously grew from a traditional hair salon to a full-service spa, a beauty store, a coffee shop, and a community space wrapped in one. Today, it no longer offers isolated customers isolated beauty services, but rather builds a well-rounded wellness experience rooted in a supportive community.

The results? Newsworthy!

Since the reinvention of the Short North and Dublin locations, **product sales went up between 35% and 65%.**

Service sales are up 10% to 44%, while "door swings" — a crucial metric measuring customer presence on premises — **are up 8% to 36%.**

No wonder why the North American Hairstyling Awards chose PENZONE as its 2019 Salon of the Year, beating hundreds of innovating brands at dozens of hot and glitzy locations.

65%
sales of products

44%
service sales

36%
"door swings"

Salon of the Year

The story of PENZONE Salons+Spas is one of remarkable bravery

When you look at a story like this one, it is easy to assume that change comes easily to some. But just because someone reinvented successfully does not mean it was easy. It is difficult, and you still get it done.

When your company has existed for a half-century, the old ways run deep. "But we've always done it this way" becomes the mantra of the old-timers. Resistance to change becomes palpable.

Says Debbie Penzone: "Some of our more tenured artists preferred Charles Penzone brand name because it is all they knew. They were proud of it, proud to be connected to the founder. But Charles himself connected with many of them, assuring that he en-dorsed this move for the company's future. That helped relieve uncertainty and tension. Instead of private spaces for hair and nail services, our new concept literally took down the walls to foster more community. Our artists resisted it — hard.

"They were afraid that it would be a detriment to their personal connection with their guests. What they didn't realize is that while open, our new spaces were designed with the human connection in mind. Instead of forty-five salon chairs in a single room, they're spaced throughout five salon spaces — making the evolution much more manageable for both artists and guests."

So, what can a company do when dealing with resistance to change?

In the case of PENZONE, the answer was communication. Whether it is talking to guests or talking to team members, it is relentless and consistent communication that became the cornerstone of the company's reinvention strategy.

Debbie illustrates:

"It was really hard. So, we really went out and talked. We got groups of people to talk together. We heard them. We listened to them. And then we shared our bigger vision: 'Seriously, who are we right now? Because that person sitting in a glass house judging everyone — that is not me. Who am I to say who is beautiful?' We started challenging the idea of who are we at our core and what do we want to stand for, what do we want to be known for. I don't want to have a fashion show which is all skinny people. Or I don't want only the models that the society perceives as 'perfect.' So, we have to talk, and we have to find a way to change, to stay relevant.

"We're so much more than just outside beauty. With the new concept, we wanted to challenge the idea of who we are and what we wanted to be known for in our future. The foundation of our business is a more holistic approach with mindfulness and self-care at the core. Daily, we strive to improve lives from the inside out. Not many in our industry have adopted this approach — but they will as it's most certainly the future for beauty."

This courage to change, to stay relevant despite all objections, is what makes PENZONE's team and its remarkable leaders a benchmark in re-invention. Now it is your turn.

Your personal take-aways

What does the story of PENZONE teach you? What can you take into your own team, your company, your industry?

Team	Company	Industry

What allowed PENZONE to successfully reinvent its existing offer into a better version of itself is a deep understanding and redesign of the *total experience* that the customer is having while interacting with the company — from the brand promise to appointment booking to arrival and check-in to the experience with the service and beyond.

What parts of the experience your customers are currently experiencing with your product or service can be reimagined, rethought, and redesigned?

	Before the product/ service is bought	During the purchase	After the purchase
AS IS			
Customer experience with our brand			
TO BE			

YOU KNOW YOUR BUSINESS MUST BE RENEWED.

BUT WHAT EXACTLY SHOULD BE REINVENTED?

Now that you are inspired by cases of others, and your creative juices are flowing, it's time to reinvent your company.

Reinvention comes in many forms. In this part of the book, I am revealing 15+ ways to create breakthrough reinventions in your business and giving specific examples to start your recovery or renewal journey.

To make it easier to use and share, we arranged the fifteen ways into a simple tool: our new Reinvention Map. Whenever you feel stuck and want to explore directions for renewal, use the map as a way to consider the full range of possibilities.

But first, a bit of a science-based background.

For many companies, reinvention doesn't come easily. Why? Our current businesses are built around keeping things largely as they are. The vast performance data available at every corner focuses predominantly on the past.

How do we move our company into the future — especially when that future is more ambiguous and uncertain than ever?

To illustrate this new competitive reality, let's look at The Conference Board's C-Suite Challenge 2019. The study asked 800 CEOs what keeps them up at night. All the most common answers focused on a fear of uncertainty, including potential recession, global political instability, and corporate inability to create new business models that dealt with disruptive technologies.

When it comes to reimagination and redesign, where do we go?

To answer this question, we will build on the research of Mohanbir Sawhney, Robert Wolcott, and Inigo Arroniz, who made a strong case that companies get themselves cornered because their view of what can be reimagined is extremely limited. Their point is echoed in the dissertation of Iztok Seljak (the CEO of Hidria, who we mentioned earlier), who also happens to be a relentless researcher.

Both studies say the same thing: Throughout history, business innovation and reinvention primarily was directed toward technical and technological development. Massive budgets, prime organizational resources, and key meetings were dedicated to developing new things within the limits of traditional R&D.

That is a very limited view.

Working with countless companies large and small, our team frequently is amazed at how BIG the playing field for reinvention is — and how little this opportunity is used throughout the world.

To ensure that this playing field becomes visible and available to you, we started with the MIT article by Sawhney, Wolcott, and Arroniz, which offered twelve ways to renew a business. Reworking and adding to their framework (thank you for the permission!), we are happy to present fifteen different ways to reinvent your business.

Should you consider new customers or enter new markets? Would reinventing your organization and culture serve as a new source of competitive advantage? Would a platform-based business model work for you? Are you inspired by a new purpose, a new *why*?

These and many other directions are here to be explored, tested, and developed. Our fifteen unique starting points for reinvention range across five areas of value creation: why, what, who, where, and how. They also can be combined into endless hard-to-imitate solutions for a true competitive advantage.

And here is the real secret: Whatever dimension of your business you decide to reinvent, it all comes back to value. Unless you are increasing and improving value creation, it's not reinvention — it's moving chairs on the sinking Titanic.

Every discussion, prototype, and line in the budget is justified only if it leads you to better value creation. With that clear, let's dive into the fifteen options.

Exploring all options
with the Reinvention Map

WHAT value are we creating

Purpose & Vision

Culture

WHERE
are we
delivering value

WHO
are we
creating for

Products & services

Brand

Platform

Network &
distribution

Solution

Markets &
presence

WHY
do we create
This value

Customers

Supply
chain

Customer
experience

Organization &
culture

Revenue streams
& value capture

Process

Business Model

HOW are we creating value

01   Purpose & Vision

INSPIRATION

After taking over the REI outdoor gear cooperative, CEO Jerry Stritzke asked his employees to come up with concrete ways for the retail company to live up to its purpose and values.

As a result, OptOutside was born. The idea is simple: "We close our doors on Black Friday. We pay our employees to get outside, instead of going to work, and invite the world to join. Because we believe a life outdoors is a life well lived."

KEY REINVENTION QUESTIONS

What purpose provides the most value for our customers, employees, suppliers, shareholders, and all other stakeholders?

What concrete actions, projects, products, and processes can help us live up to that purpose better?

What kind of vision for the year _____ will give us most energy, direction, focus, and alignment?

02   Business Model

INSPIRATION

Adobe is a software company behind many crowd favorites, including the omnipresent Photoshop.

For years, the company delivered value through a traditional retail business model: You visited a retailer (or website) and purchased your software on CD.

In 2013, the company reinvented its business model. The same products were now available as a subscription downloaded from the cloud. The company cut costs by eliminating waste embedded in packaging, retailing, and shipping. And the customers won because now it's possible to subscribe for the month they actually plan to use the software instead of paying a hefty sum upfront for owning it..

KEY REINVENTION QUESTIONS

What changes to our business model can create greater value?

Is there a business model that is more effective and efficient than the one we have?

03   Products & Services

INSPIRATION

Travel has been part of human existence forever, and we've often used some form of carrying bag, no matter how primitive. But it took centuries to make our luggage easy to move by adding wheels. That happened only in 1970 — and the reinventor, Bernard Sadow, had real trouble selling the idea. In 2015, Away reinvented the suitcase by adding a removable battery, so you could charge your phone on the fly.

Both cases — the wheels and the battery — increased the real value of the product. Sales followed.

KEY REINVENTION QUESTIONS

How can our product or service deliver better value for all stakeholders?

04   Platform

INSPIRATION

When the iPhone launched, Apple had the option to serve as the singular developer of all the phone's apps. Instead, Apple allowed any developer the opportunity to use its platform to sell his or her app. As a result

- Countless developers from the most remote locations got an opportunity to reach an affluent global customer base with few barriers to entry.

- iPhone users got a chance to get even their most unusual needs met. (Forgot where you parked your car? There is an app for that!)

- Apple got a new revenue stream with a low upfront cost and no risk. Imagine actually having to hire an army of developers and marketers to meet every customer need? Instead, the platform format allows Apple to stay away from all that cost as well as the risk of app failure.

Everyone wins.

KEY REINVENTION QUESTIONS

How can we provide a platform for new offerings or solutions?

Where can we serve as a matchmaker, a unifying framework, or a common access point for others?

05   Custom-made Solutions

INSPIRATION

A number of industries – consulting, architecture, software design – focus entirely on developing and delivering unique solutions that never repeat from customer to customer.

But the growing number of mass-market companies are reinventing their products using the power of custom-made solutions. Nike offers extensive customization of shoes to its end consumers (I put secret messages inside mine). BUILD-A-BEAR toy company invites you to design your own toy. Much of Chipotle's fast-food chain popularity is attributed to its highly customizable menu. Could customization be your next winning move?

KEY REINVENTION QUESTIONS

How can we introduce customization to our products?

What can we do to solve the customer problem end-to-end, combining products and services (ours as well as those created by others) into a solution that helps them with their specific needs?

06   Customers

INSPIRATION

Our very first online course, Breakthrough Reinvention, launched in 2019, serves as a perfect inspiration for your customer-centered reinvention.

Originally we envisioned this course for ambitious change makers who work in large corporations. Once we did our first set of potential customer interviews, another segment emerged that we were neglecting and underserving: consultants to big companies.

So we designed the course to meet the needs of both employees and consultants. As a result, both groups win as they begin speaking the same language, and we win by delivering more value to more people.

KEY REINVENTION QUESTIONS

What customer needs and pain points have we not fully addressed yet, and how can we address them?

What ignored customer segments should we begin to focus on?

07   Customer Experience

INSPIRATION

The case of Penzone, which you read earlier, is a perfect story of customer experience re-invention. To inspire you to consider this reinvention option, let me give you a bit of data.

Forrester Research has a Customer Experience (CX) Index, where it rates public companies in the S&P 500 according to their CX performance. For 2018, the findings are clear: If you are a broker, invest in companies with great customer experience. "A one-point improvement in CX Index score can yield $19 billion more assets under management for the average multichannel brokerage and $6 billion more assets for the average direct brokerage."

KEY REINVENTION QUESTIONS

How can we redesign the way we work with the customer across all touchpoints, starting when they are not yet our customers?

08   Revenue Streams & Value Capture

INSPIRATION

Hotels traditionally deliver value through guest rooms and events. But what do you do with unused capacity?

Using LiquidSpace platform, a number of hotels have reinvented their way out of this problem by turning their unused rooms into a pop-up co-working space. New value delivered to the new customer equals new revenue stream. And you don't have to be a hotel to follow this path: Chances are your company has some unused offices of its own.

KEY REINVENTION QUESTIONS

How can we improve the way we get paid or find ways to get more revenues from the same resources?

09   Processes

INSPIRATION

Each day Google serves 200,000 meals throughout the company's office cafes, and much of that food is wasted. A simple process reinvention has allowed Google to prevent six million pounds of food going to landfills or compost. How did it do that?

In 2014, the IT giant partnered with an amazing reinvention pioneer, Leanpath, a company that helps track food waste and trains chefs on how to use such data. Just the fact of collecting the data created immediate change, which was further deepened by improvements in food orders and repurposing. Lower costs, greater employee motivation, and a more sustainable world all followed.

KEY REINVENTION QUESTIONS

How can we rethink our processes to increase efficiency and/or effectiveness?

10   Organization & Structure

INSPIRATION

Arizona State University took the challenge of redesigning its organizational structure to "move away from a faculty-centric culture to a student-centric culture." A practical manifestation of this idea is the new integrative life sciences school that includes philosophers, policy analysts, scientists, and ethicists all under one roof. The design has no traditional academic departments. The results speak for themselves: While many universities struggle with high dropout rates, ASU nearly doubled its four-year graduation rate.

KEY REINVENTION QUESTIONS

How can we organize ourselves better?

What structure and organizational design will allow us to deliver better value or deliver value better?

11   Supply Chain

INSPIRATION

Zipline, a San Francisco -based company, utilizes delivery drones for moving medical sup-
plies to health clinics where they are needed in multiple countries. Reinventing the way
goods are dispatched in countries such as Rwanda, it offers national-level precision delivery
with electric drones that are overseen by locally recruited and trained talent. A combination
of high-tech startup, drone manufacturer, logistics service provider, and public health system consultant, Zipline reinvented the supply chain industry to turn crisis into opportunity.

Reinventing your supply chain does not need to start with such a big leap.
Take inspiration from one of many supply chain tweaks by Zara, a fashion company. Zara
ships its products on the hangers, which allows the designs to be displayed more quickly,
thus gathering faster feedback on what sells and needs to be produced in greater quantities.

KEY REINVENTION QUESTIONS

**What can we improve or reimagine in our
supply chains?**

12   Markets & Presence

INSPIRATION

Farmer's Fridge took on the healthy meal market by asking itself a transformative question: Must a fresh ready-to-eat chef-curated meal be available only at a fancy restaurant?
Borrowing from the ubiquitous vending machines, the company developed the concept of
free-standing self-service vending fridges placed at airports, schools, and hospitals. Fresh
salads, bowls, breakfasts, and snacks can now be bought where only chips and sodas were
available before. With hundreds of machines already in operation, in 2019 the company
raised $30 million in Series C, bringing its total funding to $42 million – and expanded into
a 50,000-square-foot production facility on Chicago's South Side. Reinventing your market presence has a lot of benefits.

KEY REINVENTION QUESTIONS

**How can we reimagine the way we become pres-
ent and available to our customers?**

**Are there new distribution opportunities and
points of sale?**

**Can we rethink how customers buy or use our
products, services, or solutions?**

13   Network & Distribution

INSPIRATION

Sawhney, Wolcott, and Arroniz offer a great inspiration for this reinvention option. "Traditionally, CEMEX offered a three hour delivery window for ready to pour concrete with a forty-eight-hour advance ordering requirement. But construction is an unpredictable business. Over half of CEMEX's customers would cancel orders at the last minute, causing logistical problems for the company and financial penalties for customers. To address that, CEMEX installed an integrated network consisting of GPS systems and computers in its fleet of trucks, a satellite communication system that links each plant, and a global Internet portal for tracking the status of orders worldwide. This network now allows CEMEX to offer a twenty-minute time window for delivering ready-to-pour concrete, and the company also benefits from better fleet utilization and lower operating costs."

KEY REINVENTION QUESTIONS

Does our relationship with customers depend on a network, or should it?

If it does, how can we improve our relationships with the network and increase value for all involved?

14   Brand

INSPIRATION

Using your brand as a launchpad of reinvention can come in many forms.

First, there is "simple" rebranding. Take Burberry, a U.K. fashion brand established in 1856. After years of reinvention that included going digital and limiting the famous plain print to only 10% of the products, the company culminated the efforts with 2019 visual rebranding.

A different way to reinvent your brand is co-branding. Target was just another low-cost retailer until it focused on creating unique yet affordable co-branded collections with world-class premium designers including Philippe Starck, Isaac Mizrahi, Rodarte, Missoni, and Victoria Beckham.

A brand also can become an asset on its own. EasyGroup is an excellent example of this approach. As an owner of the "easy" brand, the company used it to enter a range of businesses across different industries, including easyJet, easyCar, easyInternetcafé, easyMoney, easyCinema, easyHotel, and easyWatch.

KEY REINVENTION QUESTIONS

How can we strengthen the story our brand tells? What additional value can we create using our brand? Is it time for rebranding?

15 Culture

INSPIRATION

Netflix, a company celebrated for its unique and powerful culture, has reinvented many aspects of its organizational culture. Before going public, for example, the company had a standard vacation policy for all employees, but no tracking system. Employees tracked their own days off and simply notified their bosses when they'd be out.

When the company went public, auditors insisted on implementing a formal tracking system. Instead, Netflix went in the opposite direction: "Salaried employees were told to take whatever time they felt was appropriate. Bosses and employees were asked to work it out with one another." The culture of freedom and responsibility has allowed Netflix to become the market leader and a giant disruptor we all love.

KEY REINVENTION QUESTIONS

How can we evolve our culture to create even more value for everyone involved?

Now that you have a sense of possibilities, let's use them to reinvent your company — or that of your clients.

So here is your task:

01. Review the fifteen ways to reinvent and the three options that show the most potential to you.

02. Brainstorm potential answers to the key reinvention questions offered for each of the chosen options. You can do it alone or together with your team/client.

03. Choose the most promising ideas and design an action plan for taking it further.

Remember, reinvention is not a spectator sport. You have to start putting theory into practice. Start today.

Selected options

Key questions

Your reinvention ideas

BREAKING THE MYTH OF INNOVATION

It happens to us at least a few times a week. We are working with a client, speaking at an event, or giving a media interview.

The usual question shows up. Why reinvention? Why not innovation?

Honestly speaking, innovation is the buzzword. It has been a buzzword for so long, it's safe to say we've developed a special cult around it.

We worship the very word. We worship the act of innovation: devising something entirely novel, disruptive, and unique. We worship the famous solutions that came as an output of innovation efforts. We worship innovators. A LOT.

We associate the idea of innovation with the famous historical figures as well as the icons of our time. We see their faces in our textbooks. We see their stories in the evening Facebook posts, encyclopedias, hundreds of documentaries, and magazine articles.

Need more names? Nikola Tesla, Albert Einstein, Steve Jobs.

Wait, there are women innovators, too. Less recognized than their male counterparts, but no less significant.

Maria Telkes invented the first 100 percent solar-powered house. Actress Hedy Lamarr helped invent technology leading to WiFi, which all of us appreciate these days. Mary W. Jackson, the first African-American female engineer at NASA, made space exploration possible. Melitta Bentz helped develop the modern coffee maker with the paper filter. Stephanie Kwolek invented bulletproof Kevlar fibers.

The list of innovators can go on and on.

Famous reinventors?

Sorry, it's hard to think of five names instantly and associate them with reinvention.

Alexander
Graham Bell

Praised for inventing the first telephone, Bell also brought to the world amazing devices such as an audiometer that helped detect minor hearing problems and gadgets that helped track icebergs in the seas or hidden treasures elsewhere.

Marie
Skłodowska Curie

A chief innovation figure, Curie was the first woman to win a Nobel Prize, the first person and only woman to win the Nobel Prize twice, and the only person to win the Nobel Prize in two different scientific fields. The Polish and naturalized French scientist received her first Nobel for the discovery of radioactivity and her second for the discovery of polonium and radium. During World War I, Curie served as the director of the Red Cross Radiology Service, treating more than an estimated one million soldiers with her X-ray units.

Reinvention simply does not have that kind of buzz.

Regardless of the specific definition of the term *reinvention,* which we'll revisit in a minute, there is no love affair. No magazine covers. No cult.

So why would we choose the word that is so far behind?

Here comes the dirty truth. (Sorry to break it to you!)

No matter how long the list of innovators gets, the data is not on our side. The law of diffusion of innovations, developed by Everett Rogers, a professor of communication studies, and popularized in his 1962 book *Diffusion of Innovations,* shows why. According to this theory and many studies and books that followed, only 2.5% of the global population are innovators. The innovators come up with new ideas and inventions to be tested by the "early adopters," the 13.5% of the world population who love trying new things and testing crazy products.

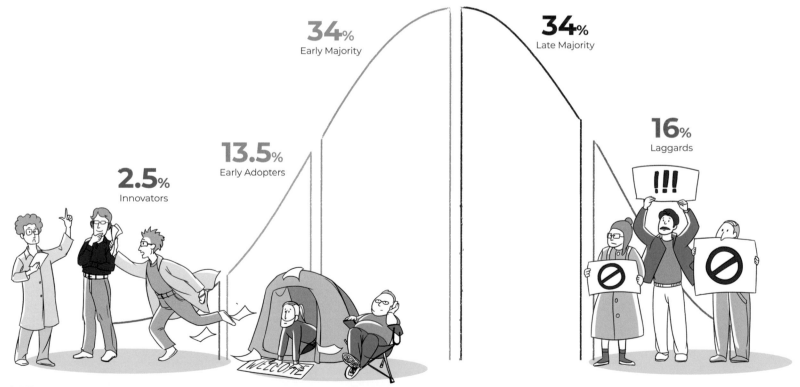

2.5% Innovators

13.5% Early Adopters

34% Early Majority

34% Late Majority

16% Laggards

The early adopters pass the message along to the "early majority," the 34% of the world population who make innovation mainstream. The late majority (another 34%) follow – and the remaining 16% are laggards, who resist any change as long as it is humanly possible.

What does this mean? Let me break it down. In a school class of first-graders, only one child potentially has the talent to invent something and obtain an original patent. College? The same. In most cases, nobody, occasionally one student, and rarely two students in a typical class have the spark to radically innovate. Enter a business meeting? No more than 2.5% of the room can innovate (if the corporate culture did not beat it out of them by now).

Whether we like it or not, this is the truth: Only a tiny percentage of us are innovators.

So when you come to your company and start glorifying innovation, for the absolute majority of people (97.5% of them, to be precise!), you are talking about something foreign, abnormal, unnatural, and scary.

Reinvention, on another hand, is within everyone's reach. It builds a bridge between the past, present, and future — as everyone can imagine a small, simple way to improve things and make them better.

2.5% are innovators

100% are reinventors

Want to prove this with an assignment?

Imagine that you are given a job for the next two hours. You need to come up with a completely new way to transport small goods. The vessel must easily store items weighing up to ten pounds (five kilograms for a majority of the world). The design also should draw praise for its aesthetics and high quality.

According to the 2.5% theory, the flashbulb will light up only in the heads of a few of you reading these words. (To be brutally honest, we don't think we would make it into that 2.5% ourselves.)

The vast majority will detest the assignment. The brain won't even bother to start thinking of a solution.

If you are a CEO who gives these types of assignments to your company's employees, expect that a substantial number of your people will just freeze. Your people will get numb, lack ideas, and grow seriously frustrated. Innovation is a very tall and nearly impossible order.

But what if we reframe the assignment?

Now look at your favorite bag or backpack.

Yes, it is a perfect vessel to transport ten pounds!

Relax. Think. Imagine.

What is the one thing you can improve on your bag?

This is the difference between innovation and reinvention.

Once you are invited to reinvent, the ideas start flowing immediately.

Innovation frames the challenges as something disruptive. An impossible ideal. A scary task.

Reinvention suggests that you can improve what you already have. Even the smallest effort counts. A better offering. A better design.

Few of us can innovate. Everyone can offer one reinvention idea. Reinvention offers every one of us and our companies a more accessible pathway.

This pathway can be harnessed by the 97.5% of the global population who are not Curie, Bell, Tsukamoto, Einstein, Lamarr, Bentz, Kwolek, or Tesla.

To reinvent is to follow a path of endless possibilities. How can we upgrade, boost, enhance, revamp, and become a better version of ourselves? Many of us can imagine improving one thing on that backpack but will fail in inventing a new type of bag.

The two assignments position the same challenge in two different ways. Innovation demands the impossible. Reinvention corrects our perception of novelty. It changes our approach to change.

As a consequence, it also changes our reaction to change. Change doesn't have to be an impossible ideal. Progress does not have to be all pain and agony. We don't have to do what is unnatural or scary.

Innovation might be the global darling, but reinvention is always the more accessible and smarter approach to change.

> **" Few of us can innovate. Everyone can offer one reinvention idea.**

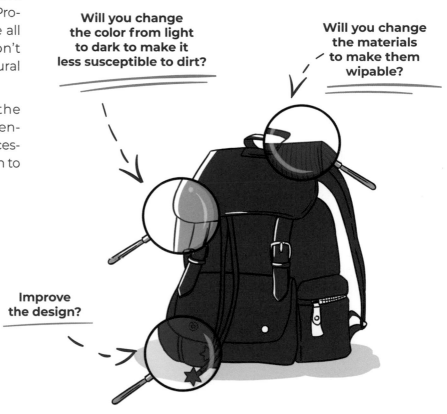

Will you change the color from light to dark to make it less susceptible to dirt?

Will you change the materials to make them wipable?

Improve the design?

FIRST, REINVENT YOUR BUSINESS MODEL

You looked at all the facts and figures, you compared your personal experience with data from the market battlefield. You are ready to take reinvention seriously.

Where do you start?

Most companies are obsessed with the technical side of things, focusing reinvention efforts on re-engineering the product or process. Technical innovation is a sexy topic, and new products are all the rage. Built into the hype is a strong assumption: To survive, you must possess the best technology, show technical savvy, or get killed.

Does this assumption hold true in the real world?

To answer this question, we come back to our old friends Kodak and Nokia. The lack of technological innovation was NOT the thing that brought down both companies. Kodak invented digital photography, while Nokia owned nearly 50% of the smart phone market at its prime.

So the technology can't be blamed for killing them. It's not as if they were producing horse carriages and got run over by the first car manufacturers.

Both Kodak and Nokia had the technology, but it did not make one bit of a difference.

What makes a difference is using old resources but imagining new and fresh ways of creating value. Let me illustrate.

Bayerische Motoren Werke AG — known to you and me as BMW — is a company widely recognized for technical innovation. It indeed produces marvelous cars. Yet today, its reinvention efforts are centered not on those technical marvels, but instead on clever ideas about how those marvels can be used differently.

To signify this shift, the company moved beyond selling products to selling services and transformed itself from a carmaker into a mobility company. Focusing on mobility, a service rather than a product, allows the company to open doors to a completely new business opportunity.

Take, for example, the DriveNow car-sharing service featuring BMW and Mini cars. The idea is simple: For anybody living in densely populated urban areas, DriveNow allows you to enjoy the benefits of a personal car without owning one.

The idea, as BMW explains, is simple: "The mobility concept is based on the motto 'pick up anywhere, drop off anywhere.' You locate the available cars using the app, website, or by just spotting the car on the street. A card or app serves as the key. You find the car, open, and drive. Once you arrive at your destination, nearly

any public parking is a place to leave the car.

The app bills you for the time you use the car — and the fee includes the cost of fuel, repairs, parking tickets, car taxes, and insurance.

It's easy, and it is fun.

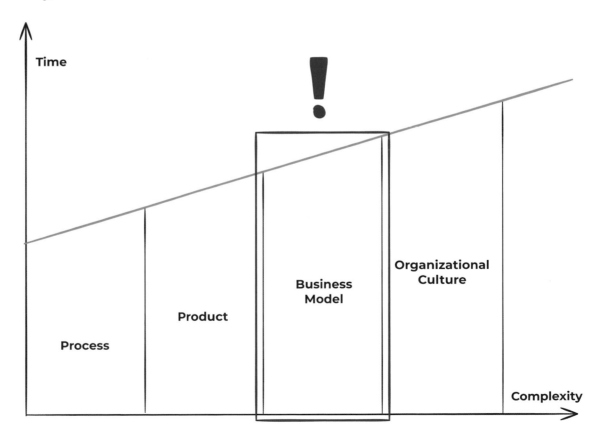

Here comes the crucial point. No new concept cars were developed for this service. Rather, the company came up with a better way to use the existing cars.

JustPark, a strategic investment by BMW i Ventures, is another example of BMW's business model reinvention. A simple online marketplace, powered by an app, JustPark allows people who own private parking places to connect with people who are searching for one.

Imagine the savings of time, fuel, CO_2 emissions, and more – plus the money made – with this simple solution.

And for BMW itself, having a stronger parking infrastructure is essential for future sales. If we have good parking, we are ready to drive cars, right?

A fifty-year-old story of Rolls-Royce is another great and surprisingly fresh example of business model reinvention. Rolls-Royce luxury cars are among the most recognizable brands in the world. However, the company makes most of its money not on cars, but its engines.

The production of powerful engines for aircrafts, ships, and other purposes is, by any means, a function of technological innovation. It is the most bricks-and-mortar (and a lot of metal) business driven by technology that you can imagine. And indeed, that is what the company produces.

But it is not what the company sells.

In 1962, Rolls-Royce developed an fresh solution to support its Viper engine. Named Power-by-the-Hour, it offers a complete service for engine and accessory replacement on a fixed cost per flying hour.

In essence, the company took a physical product and turned it into a service.

What does that mean, exactly?

Imagine you are an airline executive in charge of the fleet. Traditionally, your airline purchases all planes at full cost. The Power-by-the-Hour model, however, means that you are not paying for the engines of your new planes.

Instead, you are paying for each hour of flights.

If the engine is working, and you are making money with it, you pay.

If the engine fails, and the plane is grounded, that's Rolls-Royce's problem.

So not only do you avoid paying millions for the engine upfront, but also you avoid

> **No new concept cars were developed for this service. Rather, the company came up with a better way to use the existing cars.**

paying for any quality issues the engine might have during your ownership.

Because you do not own it.

In 2002, the company went further, and the signature Power-by-the-Hour service became part of a much-extended service offering: Rolls-Royce CorporateCare.

Among new features are Engine Health Monitoring, which tracks on-wing performance using onboard sensors, and the option to lease engines to replace an operator's engine during off-wing maintenance, minimizing downtime and costs.

Now plane operators can manage the risk related to unscheduled maintenance events, making maintenance costs predictable. Rolls-Royce gets its engines back for re manufacturing, all while churning out the same old engines. As a result, already in 2011, more than half of its annual revenues of £11.3 bil-

lion (about $17.5 billion U.S.) came from the services — not the original equipment manufacturing. That is reinvention worth paying attention to!

BMW, Rolls-Royce, and countless others invite us to put the technological innovation aside for a minute and first consider the possibility of reinventing the very business model that allows your company (your community, your organization, or yourself) to create something valuable for others.

First, reinvent your business model. Everything else will follow.

To help you with this task, we have developed a collection of twenty-five business models for you to consider, along with exercises that will help you choose the right one for your business. While there are many other business models, we chose these as the essential starter set for you to consider. Wet your business

model appetite, and more possibilities will emerge.

You'll find the full set as a special insert at the end of the book. Time to roll up your sleeves!

Building your reinvention toolkit

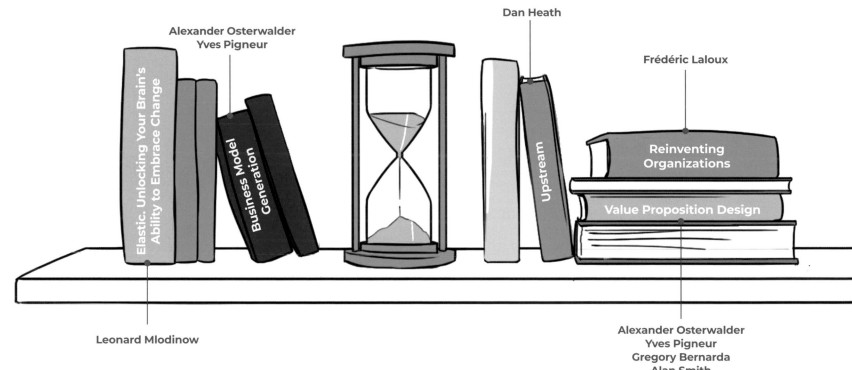

**Alexander Osterwalder
Yves Pigneur**

Dan Heath

Frédéric Laloux

Elastic. Unlocking Your Brain's
Ability to Embrace Change

**Business Model
Generation**

Upstream

**Reinventing
Organizations**

Value Proposition Design

Leonard Mlodinow

**Alexander Osterwalder
Yves Pigneur
Gregory Bernarda
Alan Smith
Trish Papadakos**

BOOKS

We continue to help you with your personal reinvention kit by featuring great books and articles on the what of reinvention. Our top picks are suggested here - and you can always get links to these resources and find even more helpful tools at **www.ChiefReinventionOfficer.com/resources**

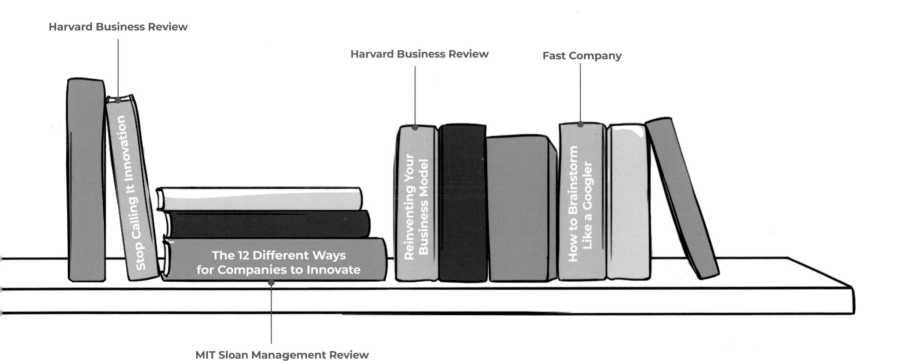

Harvard Business Review

Stop Calling It Innovation

The 12 Different Ways for Companies to Innovate

MIT Sloan Management Review

Harvard Business Review

Reinventing Your Business Model

Fast Company

How to Brainstorm Like a Googler

ARTICLES

Intelligence is the ability to adapt to change.

Stephen Hawking

PART 3

HOW

TO MAKE YOUR COMPANY WATERTIGHT

THE HOW OF REINVENTION: WHERE DO WE START?

We've explored the *why* and the *what* of reinvention. By now (I hope!) you see why the reinvention mindset, tool set, and skill set should be part of everyone's foundational education and what reinvention might look like in your business and beyond.

The question remains: How do we make it happen? How do we succeed in the present and thrive in the future? How do we reinvent today and build a system of proactive reinvention for tomorrow?

> **To avoid the natural decline, companies need to continuously renew, recreate, and reinvent themselves.**

Jumping the S-curve: The new essentials

If we translate the word *rein-vention* into executive jargon, much of it correlates to the research and practice of "jumping the S-curve."

The term of unclear origins that some trace to the management thinker Charles Handy refers to the idea that a company, product, or team life cycle can be viewed as a curve that resembles the letter "S," slightly bent.

To avoid the decline on the right side of the cycle, companies need to continuously renew, recreate, and reinvent themselves.

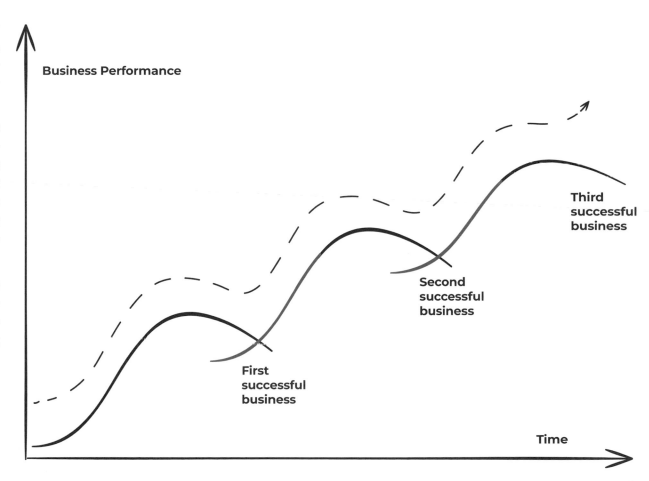

The idea of jumping the S-curve has been around for decades, with countless books and articles speaking about this secret of corporate eternity. Yet, as we have discussed throughout the book, our collective track record does not reflect that theory has successfully migrated into action, with companies expected to disappear in record time and 75% of all change efforts failing. Why are we not using this secret?

The answer, paradoxically, lies in yet another question. Most companies fail to reinvent not because they don't understand the why of reinvention or don't know what is needed in their organizations or lives. The real question of reinvention is when.

Start reinvention too late, and you are cooked. Research shows that reinventing once your performance has stalled or started to decline gives you only a 10% chance of ever re-turning to your own historical peak. The budgets get cut, the emotions run high, and the political will is not there to take one courageous experiment necessary to find a new S-curve.

You have to start the renewal while you are still growing. But here comes another catch: Start the renewal process too early, and you jeopardize the current working reality before the new version of you is viable. Often the economics are not yet there to make your new venture successful, and you are taking away valuable resources from what's already working.

The key is knowing when it is time to launch your re-invention process and staying vigilant in the face of ever-present Titanic Syndrome. For that, you need to look at **reinvention as a system** and build **healthy cycles of planned renewal** to ensure current and future viability.

Everyone's reinvention system is different. Some industries require multiple reinventions per year while others can have a healthy cycle that takes two to three years.

Some focus primarily on internal capacity while others engage external partners, suppliers, and customers.

Some organizations *(let's call them Type A)* create a separate task force or an independent legal entity, such as a corporate venture capital fund in charge of renewal.

Some create a new internal function led by a Chief Re-invention Officer or equivalent *(let's call them Type B)*. Yet others embed reinvention into all aspects of the company operations: It's considered in the strategic planning cycle, included in the budgeting, used for individual goal setting and performance appraisal, and applied throughout the business *(that's a Type C setup)*.

The ABC of Self-Renewing Organizational Design

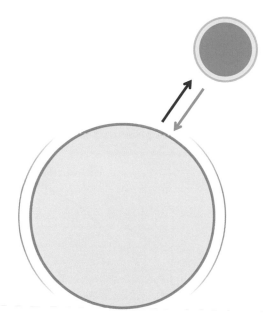

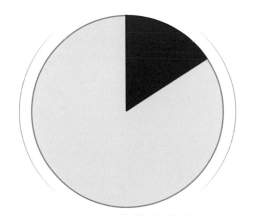

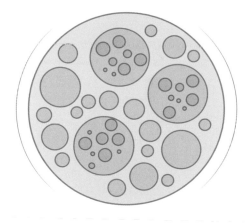

Type A

Reinvention efforts are managed by a separate task force (such as a project team) or an independent legal entity (such as a corporate venture capital fund) with significant independence and agency.

Type B

Reinvention efforts are placed in hands of a new internal function led by a Chief Reinvention Officer or equivalent.

Type C

Reinvention efforts are embedded across all functions and are built into all key systems and processes, such as planning, budgeting, hiring, performance management, and renumeration.

None of the A, B, and C types is better or worse than the others; they all fit different needs and realities. A company that has a very rigid organizational culture or highly regulated environment might do better with an A setup, keeping the distance between the incumbent business and the new venture. Another organization with heavy process orientation and a culture of continuous disruption and improvement might prefer option C.

No two reinvention systems are alike – and you will have to build one that is custom-fit for your company, industry, and reality. However, there are some foundational pieces all reinvention systems must have to assure succeeding today and thriving tomorrow. My research and practice show **six elements that are essential** to building such a reinvention system.

We call them pillars because just like the buttresses in a medieval cathedral or the vertebrae in a human body, they hold everything up. And just like the spinal column, the pillars are meant to serve their own unique purpose while reinforcing each other and the entire system of reinvention. Let's look at each element and how they all fit together.

Building your reinvention system with the Six Pillars Framework

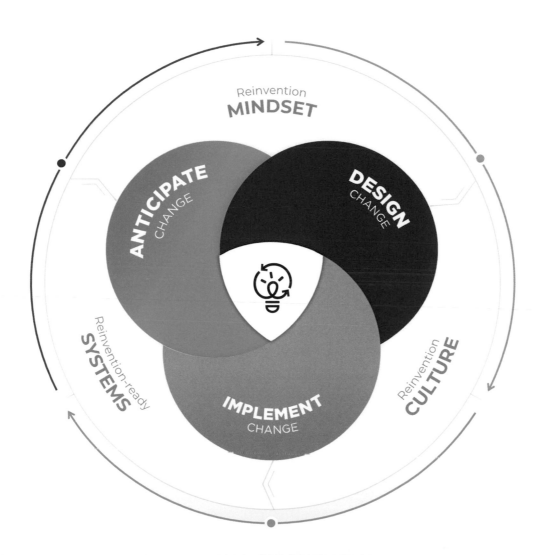

Anticipate, design, implement, then repeat

The first three pillars of the reinvention system are focused on the immediate need for renewal. Most likely you already engage in these tasks, but perhaps some of the activities happen ad hoc, are run by different departments, and are not linked to a proactive, cohesive process. Building your own reinvention system, thus, is more about aligning them into one cohesive, deliberate flow rather than doing something fundamentally new. Cross-functional, cross-boundary bridge-building is the name of the game.

Anticipating change

allows you to spot new and emerging trends before they are turned into threats or transformed into opportunities by your competitors, leaving you in the dust. Here it's crucial to go well beyond the usual channels of information.

Perhaps you already speak to customers, suppliers, and competitors as well as pick up new insights via professional magazines and trade shows. Now it's time to go beyond the usual and talk to sources that you never connected with before. Fresh eyes, fresh takes, and timely information are what we are aiming for with this step in the process.

Different companies accomplish this goal through different means. Some create a trend-watching team to collect and synthesize the most important information and share it with the organization in the most efficient way. Some engage the help of unique and previously ignored sources of information (such as www.trendwatching.com) that deliver high-quality insights that are difficult or expensive to produce on one's own. Many create a regular company-wide event to explore new directions, map out risks and opportunities, and prioritize potential icebergs, earthquakes, and storms that might disrupt the business.

One of my favorite methods of generating regular out-of-left-field insight with little to no cost is to engage a local high school or college. In every country and every community, there is an educational institution nearby with at least one teacher craving to give his or her students a chance for a real-life project. So we make a deal where every new class creates a trend report for your specific product, industry, or challenge. You'll get regular insights from an unusual source, and the students get a chance for experiential learning. Everyone wins.

Designing change

is the practice of exploring, prototyping, and testing options for the new version of your process, product, business model, and beyond.

Here is your task: Reinvention means stripping yourself of everything but your best, your very core, and elevating that best to a new form of reality. It requires you to strike a perfect balance between managing change and managing continuity. What is crucial here is this: Do not start from scratch! Keep the essence. Preserve your company's core. And then find a better way of using it.

As the art of seeing the world anew, reinvention invites you to appreciate the past and use it to discover an unexpected future. English scientist Sir Isaac Newton spoke about this ability beautifully when he reflected on his experience: "If I have seen further than others, it is by standing upon the shoulders of giants." To reinvent, stand on the shoulders of all who came before you and look for new horizons.

There are many methods and schools of thought that might help you with this part: design thinking, customer development, Appreciative Inquiry, and more. The most important thing to know about the successful design of change is simple: Participation. Let me illustrate it with a study.

Picture this.

It's 1947, and in the small town of Marion, Virginia, at the Harwood Manufacturing Corporation's pajama factory, a bit of magic is taking place.

All workers are divided into four very similar groups and are asked to change the way they do things.

The changes are minor — for example (and yes, this is a re-al case), folding pajamas into a box rather than on top of a flat piece of cardboard.

Yet Group One becomes extremely aggressive toward management and sees 17% quit in the first forty days. Meanwhile productivity drops immediately to about two-thirds of its historic output rate and stays at the new low level for thirty days after the change is introduced.

Group Two loses a bit of productivity right after the change is made but quickly recovers. There are no quits in the first forty days and only one act of aggression against the supervisors.

But the real miracle takes place in Groups Three and Four.

"After a slight drop on the first day of change, the efficiency ratings returned to a pre-change level and showed sustained progress thereafter to a level of about 14% higher than the pre-change level. They worked well with their supervisors, and no indications of aggression were observed from these groups. There were no quits in either of these groups in the first forty days."

From minus 33% to plus 14% — that is a measurable difference in productivity and bottom line. Actively and regularly engaging your employees in designing and deciding reinvention projects is key.

Implementing change

is all about getting things done. Making sure your re-invention actually works. Crossing the finish line. But here is the secret: Traditional command-and-control execution no longer works. Rather, we have to use the customer-centered, iterative process of "prototype, test, improve," advocated by such schools of thought as Lean Startup and Agile.

The essential idea is here: Start with understanding the real problem you are trying to solve for your internal or external customers or the job your customer wants to get done. Develop a wide range of possible solutions, and then treat each idea as only one hypothesis. Get on to testing, getting feedback, making necessary changes, and dumping hypotheses that did not get confirmed. (We'll give you

a cool tool to manage this process, the STELLAR Strategy Model, later in the book.) Once you have a solution that survives all tests, your reinvention succeeds — and it's time to move on to the next one!

Anticipate, design, implement, then repeat. These are the first three pillars of building a successful system of reinvention. All three are essential for addressing the disruption you are facing today, but

they are not enough. To ensure that you are also able to reinvent tomorrow, three more pillars need to be put in place: reinvention mindset, reinvention culture, and reinvention-ready systems.

Short-term survival is not enough: We must assure long-term resilience and growth

Building a continuous process that allows for anticipation, design, and implementation of needed change addresses the most immediate need for a pivot. Together, they assure the short-term survival of your product, company, or career. But as you remember from our TOTO Matrix, succeeding today is only half of the needed reinvention. Assuring that we are able to thrive tomorrow is the other half, and that's where three more pillars come in: mindset, culture, and systems of reinvention.

Reinvention mindset is a shift in the foundational beliefs about the nature of change.

Companies and leaders that survive and thrive in chaos are the ones who continuously invest in dismantling old assumptions, values, and beliefs about change and create opportunities for building a new mindset. We covered the essence of this new mindset in Part 1 when we spoke about the five flips, but how do you shift somebody's mindset?

Start with awareness. Naming the beliefs and unspoken assumptions brings everything into the open and invites your team/family/community to explore. Perhaps those beliefs were crucial and beneficial twenty years ago, but today they are holding you back. It's time to let them go!

In our global Reinvention Society, this is done in many different formats. Running a series of Titanic Syndrome sessions, hosting regular Reinvention Breakfasts, giving people a chance to taste new beliefs via data, exercises, pilot projects — all work well. The key is giving everyone a chance to consciously choose the beliefs best fitting the needs of the present rather than to be controlled by the unconscious choices made in the distant and different past.

Reinvention culture helps with that task. As a collective representation of deeply held beliefs, culture manifests itself in the way we think and

act. What kind of work environment have we created? What kind of actions do we celebrate or punish? What rituals do we preserve, and what have we dismantled?

You can think of organizational culture as its immune system. It is a collective memory of a particular way of thinking and acting that helped the company survive and thrive in the past. Now that we are facing a very different, accelerated present — and an even more disruptive future — it's time for us to get our immune system ready for it.

So what helps? An environment in which change is celebrated, experiments are encouraged, and failing is not frowned upon. In my recent Harvard Business Review article titled *Three Things You're Getting Wrong About Organizational Change,* I've shared a few examples of reinvention-friendly rituals and behaviors you might consider.

One of them is running a full-on Fail Party or a short embarrassment warm-up before your next meeting. "Scientists from the Kellogg School of Management in the U.S. ran a series of experiments to see what kind of warm-up leads to a better, more productive brainstorming session. In one such experiment, managers were put together into small teams to generate unusual uses for a cardboard box. Prior to brainstorming, however, half of the groups were instructed to share an embarrassing moment from the past six months, and the other half to share a proud one.

"The results were clear: Teams that shared embarrassing stories generated 26% more ideas than groups that shared stories of pride... The teams that shared embarrassing stories also generated a wider range of ideas, spanning 15% more categories."

Another example is organizing a Kill Your Company exercise. In addition to building a strong reinvention mindset and culture, it can help with anticipating change in a timely manner. "You bring together a diverse group of employees (and occasionally engage suppliers, customers, and young students), divide them into groups, and ask them to brainstorm the most effective and efficient ways to kill the very company they are assembled by.

At the end of a typical Kill Our Company day, the range of diverse ideas of how to kill (and save) the company is matched only by people's willingness to change in order to avoid the unfortunate fate. Lisa Bodell reports, "The first time HBO did this exercise, it generated three pages of tactics that a top competitor could use to destroy its network. An American mining company runs this exercise regularly to protect itself against both competitive and market forces. A city council in Texas even repurposed it as Kill the Community to identify and address potential threats to their city."

Many other options exist, and our final Reinvention Case for the book, which you'll find in a few pages, will illustrate how a particular ritual can drive reinvention mindset and culture in a very traditional manufacturing environment. It does not matter what specific option you choose. It matters that you actually get a new culture going.

Finally, the sixth pillar: **reinvention-ready systems.** The idea is simple. You might have every good intention in the world to adapt, pivot, and reinvent — but if your information tech, finance, operations, logistics, and other systems do not allow flexibility, all your efforts are for nothing.

Take traditional budgeting, for example. Being flexible and responsive to new market conditions sounds great — until you try to correct your company (department's or business unit's) course in the middle of the year. Suddenly all the lofty agility slogans are crushed against the reality of a static and rigid annual budget, which allows only small variations, if any, and cannot assess any significant impact, or lack thereof, of any decisions.

One of my long-term clients, a global commodity business with a diversified portfolio of products, used to follow the tradition of public companies. It assembled an annual budget in three rounds between September and November, and the board approved the final budget in early December.

One year it happened that only a month after the budget approval, in the first days of the new year, its core commodity was trading at minus 80% of the anticipated price. There was no simple process to recalculate the annual budget to reflect the losses. The company was damaging its entire business but had no ability to adapt its course quickly.

Now the same business operates with a rolling 18-month budget that dynamically adapts its forecasts (realistic, optimistic, and pessimistic) based on incoming factual data along with new macroeconomic conditions (currency exchange rates, inflation levels, and more). The rolling reinvention-ready budget saved the day.

What systems should be rethought and redesigned in your organization to allow for continuous reinvention? It's time to get adaptive!

Fitting it all together

The six pillars are meant to work together to help you build an effective reinvention system fit for your specific needs and realities. **In ideal circumstances, your reinvention process goes in an orderly fashion and perfect sequence.**

First, you've built a thoughtful method that allows you to spot trends and anticipate change. From there, you engage your employees and other stakeholders to design possible directions for reinvention, which are added to your reinvention portfolio and go into testing and implementation. You repeat this cycle regularly as needed for your industry, company, and career. You also invest in strengthening your mindset and culture and getting your systems reinvention-ready.

To reflect this perfect dream, originally, we drew the six elements of the framework as a stable building with six strong columns. We then realized that the mindset, culture, and systems are better represented as an unshakable foundation and a beautiful protective roof. The resulting visual offered a sense of strength and stability. I still love this metaphor and treat it as aspiration. **The reality, of course, is much messier than that.**

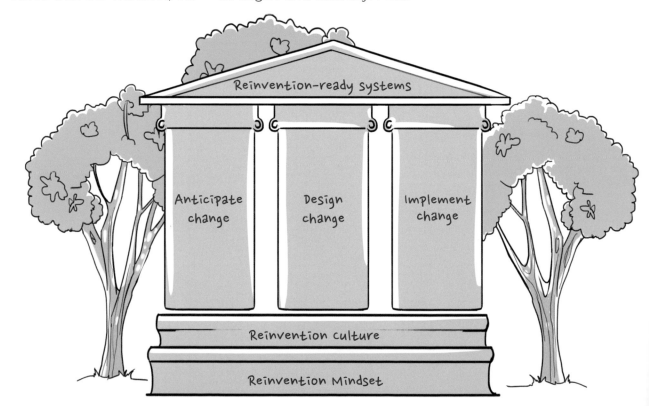

The vast majority of projects I and my team are asked to help are already in the implementation stage. Nobody spotted the trend, it turned into a full-on threat, and we are called to put out a fire. Occasionally we are invited to deal with the design of change. The only repeat customers are those who think proactively and focus on prevention, asking to build a full system.

We've seen companies suffer from implementing only a few of the six pillars. Take the first three pillars, for example. I've seen companies with strong anticipation of change efforts and strong development of design capabilities but weak implementation. As a result, nothing gets done (except for a growing sense of change fatigue).

In some companies, particularly family-owned businesses, the owner goes straight from anticipation to implementation and bumps into strong employee resistance and poor solution design. Others focus on design and implementation but always lag behind the big trends, forever defensive, late, and reactive.

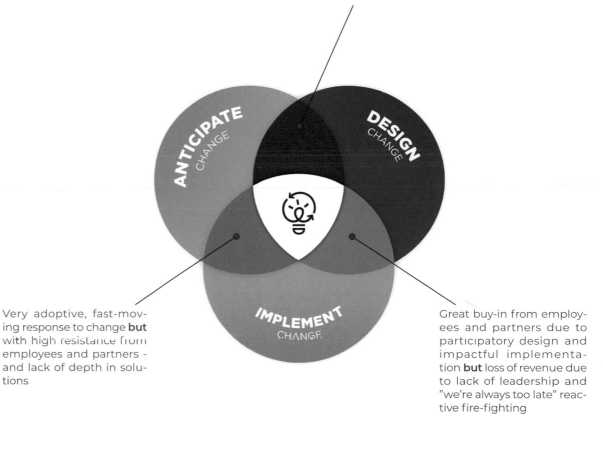

Potential first mover advantage due to proactive trend-watching and thoughtful design **but** loss of trust and revenue due to poor implementation

Very adoptive, fast-moving response to change **but** with high resistance from employees and partners - and lack of depth in solutions

Great buy-in from employees and partners due to participatory design and impactful implementation **but** loss of revenue due to lack of leadership and "we're always too late" reactive fire-fighting

The path toward a fully functional reinvention system is complex, iterative, and unpredictable. That's the bad news.

The good news: You can start at any point, enter the process with any of the six pillars, and still be useful, relevant, and impactful. Here's even more good news: You never have to reinvent the wheel (pun intended). Countless tools for reinvention exist already. The problem is that businesses rarely use these tools – and when they do, they are not built into a cohesive process. Why? Most of the time, the managers in these businesses work inside functional silos, with much of their efforts dedicated to short-term results.

In contrast, reinvention is a cross-functional effort that works across different time horizons, including short-, medium- and long-term results. Working across functions, silos, and time horizons requires an entirely different set of skills, including strategy, economics, foresight, design thinking, agility, continuous improvement, change management, organizational development, leadership, and many others.

Numerous schools of thought have worked on methodologies that comprise the tool kits for each or all of the six pillars of the reinvention system. Trend analysis, scenario planning, Appreciative Inquiry, Future Search, resiliency surveys, IDEO methodology, Agile, SCRUM, Jobs-To-Be-Done, Business Model Generation – the list is long. That's why my team and I decided to focus on developing a short list of new tools and frameworks, featured throughout this book – and only if we could not find something that already exists and works well.

The crucial thing is to connect all six pillars and focus them ruthlessly on the task of elevating strengths and reinventing value.

Do not start from scratch. Discover the rich buffet of tools and tricks already created, and then add on to make a plate fit for your specific tastes.

Do not start from scratch. Discover the rich buffet of tools and tricks already created, and then add on to make a plate fit for your specific tastes.

LEADERSHIP VERSUS MANAGEMENT: WHICH ONE IS MORE IMPORTANT?

Reinvention requires a carefully choreographed dance of leadership and management. Let me explain.

Whenever I work with a group of business professionals on change and continuity, what eventually gets in the way is the issue of leadership versus management. How does leadership differ from management, and more important, which one plays the leading role in the story of organizational reinvention?

Think about it. What comes to mind?

The first contender for the starring role in the process of reinvention is leadership. Many equate "leadership" with "leaders," where leadership is a group of people beaming charisma to inspire people throughout the organization. But if we look beyond the formal positions and titles, it is clear that all of us act as leaders sometimes. Inventing fun ways to inspire your two-year-old daughter to brush her teeth is a typical leadership activity. So is encouraging your co-worker to take a risk with an upcoming client presentation. Leadership in this sense is all about helping others (and if needed, oneself!) to deal with change in the most productive way. Because reinvention is all about change, it seems logical that leadership should play the most important role in the process of organizational renewal. Or should it?

The second contender for the leading role in the process of reinvention is management. Again, if we look beyond titles and positions, management is something all of us perform every day. Remember brushing your teeth? If teaching a child a new hygiene habit is a leadership activity, brushing your teeth as a part of an established, organized and well-performing morning routine is a management activity. So is organizing a progress meeting for the difficult project or streamlining the existing manufacturing process. In essence, management is all about helping yourself and others to simplify complexity, to take a scattered and chaotic situation, and to organize it so it becomes bearable. It is hard to imagine successful reinvention without this difficult job being done well.

So which one — leadership or management — is more important when it comes to reinvention?

The answer is simple: both. Leadership and management cannot be separated from each other, as they are deeply interrelated. Here is how.

**" Since reinvention is all about change, it seems logical that leadership should play the most important role in the process of organizational renewal.
Or should it?**

The central task of leadership is to overcome the comfort of complacency and invite the organization into change long before the need for change becomes visible. If leadership is done right, the result is **a healthy chaos:** The old system is being dismantled, and the new is being built.

The central task of management is taking the chaos created by all that change and reordering, simplifying, and organizing the complexity until none is left. If management is done right, the result is **a healthy, normal stagnation:** All systems are running smoothly, and stability is reigning. And to avoid a slide into unhealthy decline, just about then it is time to start changing again!

Thus, for reinvention to produce desired results, both are crucial: Leadership inspires us to start on a new climb, while management assures us that everyone makes it to the summit. Leadership demands that we dream big, while management guarantees that our dreams are translated into practical reality. Leadership drives change, while management safeguards continuity. If one is done for too long without the other, the organization is doomed. When both are done in a consistent cyclical manner, such a Reinvention Cycle allows for a healthy and systematic renewal.

Here is an example.

My father owns a construction business and has a passion for renovation. Fortunately or unfortunately for his family, this means that he starts reinventing our family home just for the sake of it. The last time I visited the house, I was shocked to discover that all windows on the first floor were missing, and the family was living upstairs while replacements were put in.

That is our usual story: Walls are relocated, windows are removed, and the floor is replaced.

If my father was the only one running the family, our house would constantly be under construction, with chaos and confusion at every corner.

My mother, however, loves order and stability. She cleans and organizes every evening after the crew is gone — and manages the house between renovations.

If my mother was the only one running the family, the house would be meticulously organized every day without a single change for years, with stagnation and degradation at every corner.

However, together my parents worked out a perfect cycle of leadership and management, alternating between healthy chaos and healthy stagnation for the healthy revitalization of our home.

So if you want to survive the relentless speed of reinvention required of you today, learn the art and science of both leadership and management — and connect the two into a healthy Reinvention Cycle. Healthy renewal will follow.

> **Leadership demands that we dream big, while management guarantees that our dreams are translated into practical reality. Leadership drives change, while management safeguards continuity. If one is done for too long without the other, the organization is doomed.**

Building your Reinvention Cycle

Tool #7

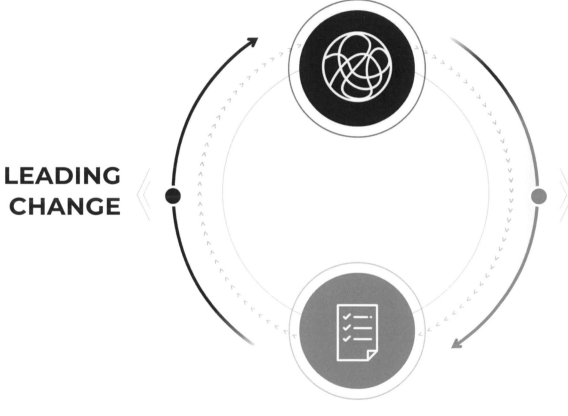

HEALTHY
CHAOS

LEADING CHANGE

MANAGING COMPLEXITY

NORMAL
STAGNATION

It's time to build your custom-made Reinvention Cycle

I hope I have made a strong enough case for building a healthy Reinvention Cycle.

As a part of your unique system of reinvention, your cycle will be different from mine.

Every company, every industry, every region is unique and particular — and requires the thoughtful design of a custom-made cycle. What works for one reality will be a disaster for another. This is not a templated solution; it has to be individual and tailor-made.

Here are the steps to get you there.

Step 1

Draw a picture of the cycle and have a conversation with your team/client about where you are in that cycle today.

If you are thinking of your personal reinvention, this is a great conversation to have with your family, friends, and colleagues.

Whether we are talking about organizational or individual reinvention, you might gain surprising and valuable insights if you ask your counterparts to mark where they see you in that cycle.

As you put the marks on the cycle, you might notice curious things: The people engaged in the conversation might put the marks in different places. What does that mean? Does it mean that they are incompetent or confused?

In most cases that is not the case: Simply put, they are living in different parts of the cycle.

We often assume that every department and every person transforms and reinvents in unison. But real life is always messier and more complex: Often multiple reinventions co-exist in the same company. Each individual reality needs to be recognized and honored as different moments in the cycle require different focus from everyone involved.

Actually mark the precise spot on the cycle with an X or any other mark — and ask everyone engaged in the conversation for the rationale.

Why did they choose that particular spot?

Step 2

Once you have clarified where exactly you are in the cycle now, it is time to clarify what is most needed from you and your team.

LEFT SIDE	RIGHT SIDE

The left side of the Reinvention Cycle is all about leading change.

Essentially what is needed here is to move the system in a way that makes reinvention inevitable. You are trying to blow up some of the existing processes, assumptions, and solutions — then clear the way for the new and better approach.

It is tempting to think that the result of a successful reinvention is a beautiful, shiny new order.

That is simply NOT possible.

Every birth in personal or organizational life is messy. There is no way to make it function like a clock with order and precision.

The result of a healthy transformation is a normal healthy chaos — where the old is already dismantled, but we are not sure yet how the new product will perform, how the new IT systems will function, or how the new performance management approach will turn out.

But we made the leap and gave birth to it anyway.

The right side of the Reinvention Cycle is all about managing the results of that birth, that explosion, that messy transformation.

Here you are trying to organize and simplify — to clear up everything that was broken, reorganized, and realigned along with everything that needs to be reset as a result of the transformation.

For those of you who love blowing things up, this part of the Reinvention Cycle might feel boring, less glamorous, or simply unimportant.

And that's where the danger lies.

I see countless companies that fail to complete this part of the cycle — jumping onto the new wave of transformation without solidifying the results of a previous wave.

As a result, the foundation becomes shaky.

The system does not get enough time to heal and realign. The employees become overwhelmed, exhausted, and discouraged.

So it is crucial to honor both sides of the Reinvention Cycle. Once you know where you are in the cycle now, prioritize and organize your activities around the needs your company has at this particular moment.

Based on where you are in the cycle, what is required from you and your team the most? Leading change or managing complexity?

How should it look exactly? What activities, initiatives, and decisions would be most impactful at this point?

Step 3

Now that you are clear about your present needs, it is time to look into the future.
In the long run, a healthy Reinvention Cycle is repeated, again and again, creating
a spiral of upward movement in the evolution of your business or your life.

Now the question is: How should this cycle look in the future?

How long should it take?

Can you put the actual timeline alongside and list specific goals you have for the next spin?

MANAGING YOUR REINVENTION PORTFOLIO

By this point in the book, we've covered a lot of ground. If there was only one thing, one main point to underline so far, it would be this: Reinvention cannot be a one-time project. As the world continues to accelerate and evolve, no singular leap of genius, no matter how great it was at the moment, is enough.

As I am writing these words, Brooks Brothers, a legendary work suit manufacturer, announced its upcoming bankruptcy. So did the car rental giant Hertz, which also rents cars under brands Dollar, Thrifty, and Firefly. Cirque du Soleil, the darling of the Blue Ocean Strategy movement (a popular strategic school of thought of the twenty-first century), announced cutting 3,500 jobs as a part of the deal to avoid bankruptcy. Your past success is not a guarantee of your future glory.

That's why it is crucial to manage a whole portfolio of reinvention efforts. In doing so, you assure diversification, allow for proper testing of hypotheses, and have a big-picture view of where to put your focus and resources.

The Reinvention Portfolio Canvas helps with this task.

The horizontal axes focus on **the scale** of your reinvention efforts. You have three options to choose from: sub-system, system, and eco-system. If you are in the automotive business, reinventing a sub-system means that you focus on just a part of a system, for example, a car transmission. Changing the entire car concept constitutes reinvention of the system. And if you are rethinking everything, including redesign of gas stations and redo of the supplier system, you are reinventing an entire eco-system.

The virtual axes focus on **the intensity** of your reinvention efforts, from incremental to intermediate to radical transformation. Tweaking a production process constitutes incremental reinvention, but completely redesigning it is radical.

Looking at the two axes, you might ask about potential metrics that can help you decide where you place the project on the canvas. The bad news: It all depends on your specific industry, company, and reality. The good news: The canvas facilitates and catalyzes team alignment as positioning the specific efforts on the canvas requires that all of you first agree on definitions and metrics.

" It is crucial to manage a whole portfolio of reinvention efforts. In doing so, you assure diversification, allow for proper testing of hypotheses, and have a big-picture view of where to put your focus and resources.

Reinvention Portfolio Canvas

Project

Date

REINVENTION INTENSITY

Radical

Intermediate

Incremental

Sub-System

System

Eco-System

REINVENTION SCOPE

Using the canvas:
Get inspired, make it yours

In our practice, I've used the Reinvention Canvas in many different ways and been inspired by the different approaches developed by our global community.

Often, I **use the canvas as a part of the organizational audit** (along with the Titanic Syndrome Survey and other steps). Working with a global insurance company recently, we started with the CEO, putting all of it on one huge wall-size canvas. It helped the company align on definitions, have difficult conversations about whether the portfolio is in healthy shape and how the company might assess its health, and notice key reinvention patterns between countries and business units.

Other times, the **canvas plays a key role in strategic planning efforts.** The company was asked to draw up its desired portfolio, the "To Be" version of the ideal collection of reinvention projects. Then the "As Is" version was created as the first step to map out a path from where the organization is today to where it wants and needs to be tomorrow.

The Reinvention Canvas also can come **handy in your project management** efforts. Having the canvas visible and accessible for the entire team facilitates clarity and focus. Teams have used different colors for different projects to reflect priority. When new projects were proposed, having one unified snapshot

of the mass of transformation efforts assured that resources were not spread too thin. If a new project comes on, then something must come off, or resources must be increased, or the schedule must be adjusted. Transparency, clarity, and focus win the day.

These are just a few examples for the use of the Reinvention Canvas. I am sure you will come up with many more ways to put it to work for you. This particular tool can be used alone or in harmony and alignment with others covered in this book.

How do the different tools fit together? What is the relationship among the S-curves, the Reinvention Cycle, and the Portfolio Canvas? Why

does one tool say that stagnation is dangerous while another suggests it's healthy?

To answer these and other questions, we've put together a free video series, along with other resources. You are invited to explore it all online at **www.ChiefReinvention Officer.com/resources**

I've used the Reinvention Canvas in many different ways and been inspired by the different approaches developed by our global community.

DANFOSS TRATA

24 hours to change the world

With the ever-increasing speed of change and the shortening of life cycles, we all need to find new ways of delivering value and reinventing our businesses on a continuous basis. Often, we get stuck not only with anticipating change and coming up with ideas to turn it into opportunity, but also at developing them and bringing them to life.

How would you feel about being able to develop a new idea for your business in just twenty-four hours? What about getting a new product delivered in one hundred days?

BEFORE

Product improvement and development took 2-3 years

AFTER

A new patent for the winning idea was filled within 100 days

How it all started

Part of the Danish-based, family-owned Danfoss Corporation for more than twenty years, Danfoss Trata is the world's leading supplier of energy-efficient solutions for remote heating, cooling, and air conditioning of buildings. As in any corporation, Danfoss Trata had some mechanisms in place for sharing and sourcing ideas from its nearly 400 employees. But in 2015, it took a sharp turn upward when a team of three enthusiasts came up with an entirely new way of encouraging entrepreneurship and innovation from within.

Mateja Panjan (then an internal communications manager) and two of her colleagues worked around the clock to bring to life their idea of a new internal innovation event that applied startup principles to a corporate setting. Driven by passion, they used their time off work to explore the idea, to present it to the Danfoss Trata leadership team, to get support to invite external experts to learn from, and to develop a project that would facilitate rapid idea development for new business opportunities and growth.

Their hard work paid off, and in June 2015, the 24idea project came to life.

Eighty employees from the Commercial Controls business came together to brainstorm on ideas for product and process improvements within the Danfoss heating segment. This pilot event was run simultaneously in Slovenia and in China, with a virtual exchange of ideas between the two hubs and facilitation by a startup expert and the 24idea team.

Starting at 2 p.m., the clock was ticking, and the teams had 24 hours to get from idea formulation, through idea development supported by mentors, to a final pitch. The air was filled with contagious energy and excitement as the hours progressed until everyone held their breath for the announcement of results after the final pitches. It's no surprise: The best team got the green light, full support, and resources from the company's management to go ahead with the idea implementation as fast as possible. And eight teams got the opportunity to spend 20% of their working time on developing new ideas and potential. This was unprecedented in company history!

The result? A new patent for the winning idea was filed within one hundred days from the moment the idea was pitched to management. Until then, product improvement and development could take as long as three years.

The effort yielded more than product or process improvement. 24idea demonstrated a massive boost in employee empowerment and engagement. Anyone could contribute ideas, get noticed, learn from colleagues with different functions and departments, develop new skills, think from different angles, and viewpoints, and co-create the company's future. A true reinvention in action!

Reaching far and wide

The first 24idea was so successful that six months later, the next event was held at the Danfoss corporate headquarters in Denmark, covering all Danfoss segments. Mateja's team was invited to co-create a model for faster innovation development on a corporate level.

This opened the doors to 24idea on a truly global scale. Since 2015, close to twenty events were run in Slovenia, China, Denmark, and Russia. Out of 120 proposed ideas, more than forty were approved, and more than fifteen ideas went into rapid implementation. Winning the title of Best of the Best 2016 by the American Chamber of Commerce Slovenia for the 24idea project was just the cherry on the cake.

What's great is that the 24idea format can be easily applied for any topic, industry, or task at hand. Besides specific technological and product improvement challenges, Danfoss Trata uses it to develop bottom-up solutions on a variety of issues. Currently more than thirty employees are regularly co-creating in the themes of the future of work, job rotation, the task market, gamification, and local, social, and health responsibility.

Danfoss Trata lends its expertise to other companies and industries. Using the 24idea principles, Danfoss was the initiator and host of the first HR Hackathon in collaboration with Competo, the leading headhunting agency in Slovenia, in early 2018. The HR Hackathon invited Danfoss and seven other companies to identify challenges for the future of work and to find solutions for them together. Each of the companies brought a different perspective, covering a variety of business sectors: A1 Telekom (communications provider), Siemens (electrification and digitalization), Iskraemeco (energy management), Big Bang (electronics retailer), Atlantic Grupa (food industry), Zavarovalnica Generali (insurance), and Steklarna Hrastnik (glassware). All participants were divided into diverse teams to hack specific HR challenges and solutions, while experienced mentors supported out-of-the-box thinking and idea development. The project was so successful that now it is a regular event run by Competo. Several other companies have adopted 24idea for rapid innovations internally, including in IT, retail, energy, and other industries.

In February 2020, Mateja, now Danfoss Front End and Innovation Manager, had every reason to be proud again. Danfoss 24idea ventured into yet another area for innovation: merging its core competence in district heating technologies with blockchain solutions. The Danfoss Blockchain Hackathon, run in collaboration with Blockchain Think Tank Slovenia, invited carefully selected teams from Slovenia, Serbia, Germany, Portugal, and Croatia to work on solutions for District Heating Utility networks to reuse and sell surplus heat. That might be the start of yet another trailblazing innovation curve for Danfoss!

24idea step by step

24idea demonstrated a strong track record for both internal reinvention and collaborative projects across different companies and industries. How does it actually work?

We have laid it out for you step by step. Try it out and add your own flavors!

24idea demonstrated a strong track record for both internal reinvention and collaborative projects across different companies and industries. How does it actually work?

We have laid it out for you step by step. Try it out and add your own flavors!

Step 1: Define the overall theme to be addressed.

Step 2: Identify mentors (internal or external), evaluation committee (top managers who act as sponsors to ensure further development of the ideas), facilitators (it might help to have a startup expert on board), and guests to boost motivation and add expertise during the event.

Step 3: Invite participants from all parts of the organization. They can come with or without a specific idea, may already have a team, or may create one on the spot. Encourage diverse teams to cross the functions, departments, expertise, and generation boundaries!

Step 4: All teams get 90 seconds to present their idea proposal.

Step 5: Selected ideas get to work further with mentors and experts.

Step 6: Test pitch by the teams is done in front of mock judges.

Step 7: Ideas are finalized.

Step 8: The final pitch is made in front of the evaluation committee, usually the sponsors from the executive team.

Step 9: The winning idea gets one hundred days and additional resources for rapid implementation.

Step 10: All selected ideas get a senior sponsor to ensure further development.

Sounds simple enough? It's time to try it out!

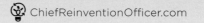

Your personal take-aways

What does the story of Danfoss Trata teach you? How can you use the idea of regular reinvention hackathons for your own personal development, your team, your company, your industry?

Self	Team	Company
✎	✎	✎

CONSISTENCY IN A VOLATILE WORLD: WHEN EVERYTHING IS CHANGING, HOW DO WE HANDLE STRATEGY?

A strategy is all about consistency. You choose a direction and stick with it.

And that brings a question: How can we approach strategy when today's world is fast, volatile, and unpredictable?

By drawing on two distinct schools of strategy — deliberate and emergent — I offer insights on how to reinvent your strategic thinking so you can use this framework with your bosses, teams, and clients.

But first things first: What in the heck is strategy?

I've been in the business of reinvention for more than twenty-five years, and I have yet to see a definition that works for all.

Businesses tweak and twist the concept of a strategy to make it work for them. Some see strategy as a collection of goals; some believe it is a detailed plan; others claim that it is all about your unique competitive position.

It is safe to say that a strategy is all of these: perspective, position, plan, and pattern.

Here is how we use this term within the Chief Reinvention Officer's methodology. You want to get from point A to point B — and there are numerous ways to do so. Your strategy is **the specific way you have selected (out of all the different possibilities!) to get from point A to point B.**

That's all.

Now that it is out of the way, the central question is how to make that decision (and stick to it!) in a world where everything changes all the time.

Your customers develop new tastes and face new pains. Your competitors push out new products. Your suppliers change pricing. Your regulators add new legal hurdles.

And change is happening at speeds we have never seen before.

 A strategy is all about consistency. You choose a direction and stick with it. But how do you stay consistent in the world that is fast, volatile, and unpredictable?

In the world of speed and uncertainty, is strategy still needed — or even possible?

Our answer is a resounding YES, but it comes with a big BUT.

To make a strategy work today, we have to move from a deliberate to an emergent framework. Instead of looking at strategy as a rigid plan, we need to create a format and a process that allows for continuous reinvention.

"There are two people whose ideas I believe must be taught to every MBA in the world: Michael Porter and Henry Mintzberg. This was true more than twenty-five years ago when I did my MBA at the University of Southern California, and it remains true today. These are two academics who have had real impact for a long time," writes Karl Moore, a McGill University professor and Forbes contributor. "Both have been very influential in the study of strategy, an area of considerable interest to many Forbes readers. You can contrast their two views as Porter's taking a more deliberate strategy approach while Mintzberg's emphasizing emergent strategy. Which one is more useful today?"

> **Instead of looking at strategy as a rigid plan, we need to create a format and a process that allows for continuous reinvention.**

Before I give you my answer to Moore's beautiful question, let's make things super-transparent: I had a chance to work closely with Henry Mintzberg while co-teaching the long-running Roundtables for Practicing Managers for a number of years. He has been an amazing help in developing ideas for my previous books. While I have never worked directly with Michael Porter, I always have used his models in classrooms and boardrooms and continue to do so whenever possible.

So this is not about kicking somebody to the curb. It is about developing strategic sophistication that our volatile world requires today.

What's the difference?

DELIBERATE STRATEGY

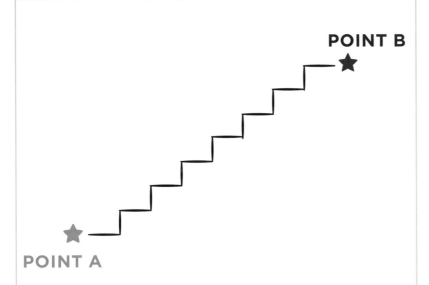

Emphasizes the role of thinking and planning before acting. Here, past performance data go through the in-depth analysis to serve as the basis of all decisions. Most important decisions are made before a single step is taken — often at a posh executive retreat with the support of an external consulting company. Once the decisions are made, implementation kicks in as a separate step of pure execution.

EMERGENT STRATEGY

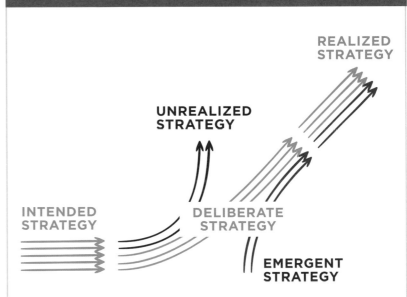

Emphasizes the role of trying and learning as a part of the strategic process. Here, strategy emerges over time as plans collide with and accommodate always-changing reality. Most important decisions are made throughout the entire process and are often based on the first set of actions taken and feedback received. As such, the emergent strategy is all about turning your organization into a place of constant learning, adapting, and re-inventing.

Now that we have clarity on the difference between deliberate and emergent strategy approaches, which one works best today?

I am sure I gave my answer away already: for a world where things move suddenly, building flexibility and re-invention into a strategic process becomes crucial.

The 2007 book by the brilliant thinker Nassim Nicholas Taleb titled *"The Black Swan: The Impact of the Highly Improbable"* introduced us to an idea of "black swan" — a high-profile, hard-to-predict, and rare event that is beyond the realm of normal expectations in history, science, finance, and technology. There is no question that such an event (if it ever happens) should significantly impact our strategy.

The key word in the definition of "black swan" is *rare*.

Indeed, decades ago, when the organizational and cultural cycles were long, and change was rare, black swans were rarely seen.

But today, the situation is drastically different. As I type these words, my team is working with a global client on scenarios that the client should be ready for: the uncertain future of Brexit, the unclear results of the U.S.-China (and the world) trade war, new threats of violent conflict in Iran, new deaths in a Sudan uprising, every kind of threat of ecological disaster from climate change to loss of species to catastrophic dwindling of forests, and much more...

Here, no matter what sophisticated analysis of the past I bet on, it says little about survival in the future.

> **Decades ago, when the organizational and cultural cycles were long, and change was rare, black swans were rarely seen. But today, the situation is drastically different. At the moment, all the swans look black.**

In other words, at the moment, all the swans look black.

That's exactly when emergent strategy comes handy. It gives you the flexibility and agility needed to adapt to a new reality. It forces you to learn with real-time data and grown competencies of organizational foresight.

Sounds good, right? But how exactly does it work?

We asked this same question years ago while working with particularly difficult reinvention cases, and we could not find a model that was pragmatic and tangible enough to fit the needs of a real business in real life. Instead of looking at strategy as a rigid plan, we needed to create a format and a process that allows for continuous reinvention.

But nothing that was available on the market fitted our needs.

So we decided to invent our own tool. Behold, our STELLAR Strategy Model!

So we decided to invent our own tool. Behold, our STELLAR Strategy Model!

STELLAR Strategy Model

Tool #9

Consisting of a set of questions to use along with a canvas (we actually offer you two different canvas options), this approach allows you to go through a sequence of decisions (sometimes iteratively) that allow you to launch and maintain a new strategic process.

To get familiar with the model, we suggest you first test this model alone as an exercise, and then bring it to your team or client organization.

1. Define your starting position, your Point A.

It might be a no brainer — you know where you are — but practice shows that different parts of the company and different leaders might see that spot very differently. Be as specific as possible and exceptionally clear on how you measure Point A. What are the defining characteristics? Is it market share? Customer satisfaction level? EBITDA (earnings before interest, taxes, depreciation, and amortization)? Anything else?

STARTING POSITION (ST)

2. Define your desired end position, your Point B.

Get down to the details on the defining characteristics of Position B: What is non-negotiable? Is it the financial aspect of the desired space? Customer segment? What mark must we hit, and what is optional?

Notice a crucial shift here: Instead of defining B as a point, we invite you to think of it as a position — an area that covers a range of possibilities.

Thinking of this as a range rather than a singular point with one set of strategic goals gives you the flexibility necessary to adapt to a changing environment. It is important to figure out your range deliberately and clearly — and celebrate when you hit any point within the defined range. If your point B is best represented by multiple goals, make sure you choose a range for each goal, giving yourself and your team flexibility and room to maneuver.

Working with a range is backed by science. Management thinker Steve Martin explains why: "High-low goals are both challenging and attainable. Researchers at Florida State University recently demonstrated how this small shift in goal setting can have an impressive impact. In one study, members of a weight-loss club wanting to lose two pounds per week were assigned to one of two groups — a single-number goal group *"lose 2 pounds per week"* or a high-low range goal group that averaged the same *"lose 1 – 3 pounds per week."* The impact of being set a high-low goal on members' sustained motivation to pursue their goal (by enrolling in an additional ten-week program) was striking. Only half assigned a single-number weight loss goal persisted with the longer-term target, but nearly 80% of those assigned a high-low range weightloss goal did."

So the range is the way to go. As you are exploring the possible ranges, make sure the ways you measure A and B are perfectly aligned. If you think that now, you are not doing a good job measuring success, and it's time to come up with a new way of measuring. What does your Position B look like, and how will you know when you get there?

END POSITION (E)

3. Using the key lessons from the past, define the limits you don't want to cross.

Many think that we constantly need to think outside the box, but as amazing creatives have pointed out, to create something new, we need to start with a box.

Limits and constraints are crucial for our creative thinking, and strategy is the best place to apply your creativity. So it is time to put down the constraints. Use the lessons from the past to guide your discussion. What kind of limits will allow you to minimize the need for micro-management and give clarity to your team? Perhaps some level of cost? Regional constraints? Customer segment constraints? What imaginary lines should your business NOT cross as it walks an emergent path from Point A to Position B?

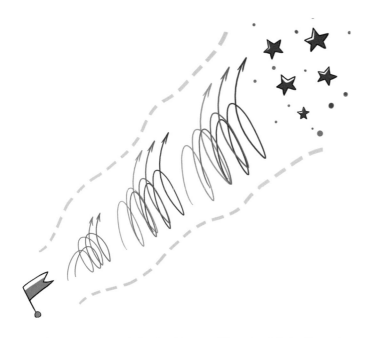

LESSONS AND LIMITS (LL)

4. Keeping in mind the desired ending position you defined in step 2 and the limits set in step 3, choose some areas of focus and the first set of actions — specific steps that you think will take you from Point A to Point B. Since reinvention is all about trial and error, you are selecting the first steps to try. If they don't work, you will have a chance to review and revise in the process.

A strong and successful strategy must take you from ideas to actions, from talk to walk, from theory to practice.

The crucial thing to remember here is this: All your actions should serve as a way of testing a hypothesis, as a way of experimenting with a question — not as a declaration of the one and only right answer.

Your first set of actions should represent a collection of different hypotheses you want to test.

Do you think product reinvention will be required to stay competitive? Begin experimenting with product changes.

Think that future competitiveness depends on entering a new customer segment? Start with testing. Perhaps a new process would offer an incredible advantage? Don't think of it as a final decision; rather think of the first actions as prototypes.

If any of the actions chosen for experiments don't work, you will have a chance to change them in the process. Testing, playing, and prototyping are the right frames of references. They allow your company to embrace agility and reinvention as part of your strategic management.

What are the first steps you can take that will allow you to run the best combination of tests and experiments? How will you measure the success of each test? And what is the KPI (key performance indicator) – or the key result expected for each action?

AREA OF FOCUS	ACTIONS (A)	KEY RESULTS
01		
02		
03		

5. Choose the date and format for your first strategy review.

Set up the first meeting for emergent lessons, revisions, and strategic course corrections. Such meetings should be held regularly at the end of a work "sprint" - which can be as short as few hours or as long as a few months.

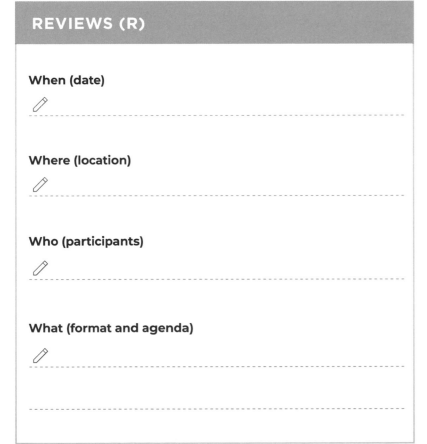

REVIEWS (R)

When (date)

Where (location)

Who (participants)

What (format and agenda)

Together, the questions help you guide the discussion while the canvas organizes the information visually and shows places of possible alignment or misalignment.

It's time to roll up your sleeves!

Option A

STELLAR Grid

Project	Date

Max

Min

Max

Min

Review

Review

🚩 Starting position (ST)

What are the defining characteristics? Is it market share? Customer satisfaction level? EBITDA? Anything else?

⭐ End position (E)

What is non-negotiable? Is it the financial aspect of the desired space? Customer segment? What mark do we have to hit — and what is optional?

★
★
★
★
★

— Lessons and Limits (LL)

Level of cost? Regional constraints? Customer segment constraints? What imaginary lines should your business NOT cross as it walks an emergent path from Point A to Position B?

➡ Actions (A)

What are the first steps you can take that will allow you to run the best combination of tests and experiments? How will you measure the success of each test — what is the KPI for each action?

Areas of focus	Actions	Key Results

— Reviews (R)

When? Where? Who? What?

CHIEF REINVENTION OFFICER METHOD

Option B

STELLAR Canvas

Project

Date

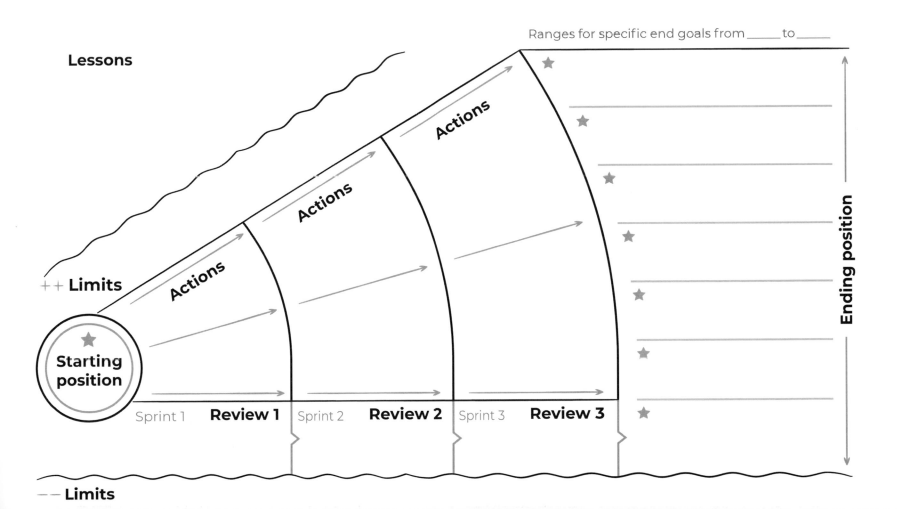

Ranges for specific end goals from _____ to _____

Lessons

Actions

Actions

Actions

Actions

++ **Limits**

Ending position

Starting position

Sprint 1   **Review 1**   Sprint 2   **Review 2**   Sprint 3   **Review 3**

-- **Limits**

THERE IS NO HOW WITHOUT A WHO

In this part of the book, we are talking about the how of reinvention. But there is no *how* without the *who*.

Reinventing our companies, products, processes, and lives is a communal affair. Doing it on your own is an exceptionally tiring, lonely, and, in some cases, dangerous journey.

As we are approaching the end of the book, it's time to start growing your change-embracing tribe.

Just as people cannot survive without a community, business ideas and strategic initiatives cannot survive without a supportive tribe. Reinvention is not an easy fix to a little problem — it takes significant time, commitment, and persistence.

You need a support system to get your company through. To share, support, ignite, grow, learn, teach, renew, vent, imagine, destroy, disrupt, and have fun in the process.

To strengthen this support system, here we invite you to do two essential things:

- Develop and nurture your **existing connections** into a more reinvention-friendly community.

- Discover and grow **new relationships** to get a greater reinvention boost and more focused support.

 Reinventing our companies, products, and lives is a community affair. Doing it on your own is an exceptionally tiring, lonely, and, in some cases, dangerous journey.

Exercise #1

Things are about to get real, so you might not like the results of this exercise. But there is no way to sugar-coat it: there are people in your EXISTING circle that are just bad for those crucial reinvention vibes. So, your task is to do a serious audit of your inner circle and get real about their impact on your reinvention efforts:

01

List 7 people that you are around the most on a daily basis

02

Assess the influence and impact each person has on your ability to embed reinvention into your life and make it a habit by circling one of the three options: **S for supportive, N for neutral, and T for toxic.**

03

Decide on the specific action you plan to take to improve the impact of each person. It might mean working more together, getting into joint projects, having some difficult conversations, or, in the worst case, it might also mean limiting the contact.

Person

Influence

Action

Person	S	N	T	Action
✎	S	N	T	✎
✎	S	N	T	✎
✎	S	N	T	✎
✎	S	N	T	✎
✎	S	N	T	✎
✎	S	N	T	✎
✎	S	N	T	✎

Exercise #2

Now that you have a clear path for strengthening your existing circle, it's time to think about finding sources of new support. Here your goal is to brainstorm and commit to clear steps you will take to boost your own reinvention efforts without any excess or overwhelm.

New reinvention support can come in many formats:

1. Engage your social media community by hosting live virtual sessions open to everyone.

2. Find a few people you want to keep connected by hosting regular Skype or Zoom virtual coffee calls to share updates and get support.

3. Find a face-to-face community that is open to all new things. Toastmasters, startup accelerators, TEDx events, etc. all suit the purpose.

4. Become more active via all the different engagement options, events, and platforms you can explore at www.chiefreinventionofficer.com/bonus.

So, let's make it real.

01

Brainstorm
the options:

✏ --------------------------------

02

Choose the option that inspires you the most and commit to real actions for making it happen:

Option	Participants	Date and Time	Next steps
✏	✏	✏	✏

Now open your cell phone and add reminders for your reinvention meetings to your calendar!

CHANGE IS NOT A PUNISHMENT

We've come to the very end of our journey together. Throughout this handbook, most of our attention was focused on reinventing your organization. But my final few words will be deeply personal.

I am a professional reinventor.

I help companies reinvent their products, their services, and their business models.

Often, I am called when things are in dire need of renewal.

Since 1994 in this line of work, my life has been filled with endless adventures and countless discoveries. Yet there are only three key lessons I learned so far that seem worthy of this moment. I offer them as the ultimate summary of all we covered – and more.

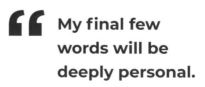

My final few words will be deeply personal.

Lesson #1

Change is accelerating, so the new starts will happen in your life more often than you can possibly imagine.

Every company, every community, and even every career goes through a life cycle.

Once upon a time, our companies, our communities, and our careers enjoyed long and healthy lives, with a slow rise to the peak of performance and a gradual decline to annihilation.

The rate of change was so slow that reinvention was rarely needed – and when it was, we had all the time in the world to renew ourselves and our organizations on our terms. But that fairy tale is long gone.

Today change happens faster than ever.

Our grandparents and even some parents used to spend their entire professional life at one organization. The latest data suggest that you will have to plan for five careers in your life – not five organizations, not five jobs, but five different careers.

Our organizations used to transform and renew themselves only once every forty years.

Today our data show that if you don't reinvent your company every two to five years, you will kill your business.

And the graveyard of companies that were big one day and dead the next is growing by the minute: Do you remember what Blockbuster was? Still have a Nokia phone lying around somewhere in the house? Have you stopped recently at the closure sale of Toys R Us?

Our lives are accelerating, and we have to face major change more often than ever before. But that is not all.

Change also comes in many new forms.

Some of it is the change you planned, wished for, and worked hard to achieve. In my own life, amazing transformations happened more often and more intensely than I could possibly imagine. Only one year after my graduation, I married the love of my life. Two years later, my daughter was born. Five years into our marriage, we launched our business, which has been growing ever since.

But more often change enters your life with no planning and no invitation. Only three weeks after my wedding day and a year after my graduation, I left for Kazakhstan to take care of my mother, who had an advanced form of breast cancer. Four years after graduation, my father-in-law killed himself. The first serious returns brought by our company were lost in a scam organized by a former friend.

So the first thing I want to say to you is this: Change will come into your life more often and stronger than ever before.

And that's where my second lesson becomes crucial.

Lesson #2

When change happens, you will have two choices: fight it or use it. Instead of fighting change, use it to reinvent.

Don't get me wrong: There is nothing wrong with fear. Fear is an important and under-appreciated emotion. Fear grabs our attention, makes us alert and focused, and prepares our minds and bodies for the battle.

But when it comes to facing most changes and disruptions, battling them or denying them is a waste of your precious energy.

Change is hard.

Annoying.

Disruptive.

Even when we had an active part in bringing the change about – starting a new job, marrying the person you actually want to marry, moving across the country or even across the world – change is confusing, draining, and painful.

Yet in a world where change is the only constant, I invite you to see it as your friend, not your enemy.

Change is an opening to try something new.

Change is an excuse to get rid of everything that no longer serves you.

Change is an invitation to design a better future.

When you embrace the disruption, when you allow yourself to let go, when you learn to ride the waves of change,

rather than be crushed by them, you earn the right to choose who you want to be.

Change is not a punishment. It is not the wrath of gods out to get you.

Change is a path to ultimate freedom. All you have to do is to invite reinvention into your life.

And this is where my final lesson comes to play.

So here it is, Lesson #3

You don't need to become a reinventor. You already are.

Facing change successfully requires us to have strong resilience, agility, and reinvention muscles.

If you worry that you might not possess those, here is a surprise: You don't need to become a reinventor. You already are.

Not only are you are a good reinventor, but also you have reinvented yourself thousands of times!

Professor Carol Dweck of Stanford University recently asked a beautiful question: Have you ever met an unmotivated baby? A baby that is simply not interested in change?

Unless it is a health tragedy, and the baby is not well, every child loves to reinvent.

I remember when my daughter, Lila, learned that she had hands. "Hooray! Two more tools I did not know I had. Time to reinvent!"

I travel all around the world. My family and I have lived on three continents. And wherever I am, no matter what political, economic, or cultural system I am in, I always see the same thing. In nearly every elementary school on the very first day, we teach our kids the same thing.

Do you have an idea of what that might be? Remember yourself, or your child, or perhaps a little brother or sister starting school?

In Ghana, Brazil, China, India, Kazakhstan, Ukraine, Slovenia, and the United States, children learn the same thing. You probably are thinking of letters, or numbers, or the name of the teacher. However, the one thing in common is this: All kids learn to sit still.

Why?

The answer is simple: They teach us to sit still for forty minutes so we can survive an eight-, ten-, or twelve-hour work day, or so we can survive a thirty-, forty-, or even even fifty-year career in the same company, doing the same job.

For centuries the world has been changing slowly. Reinvention – the natural drive that is inside of you – was unnecessary. You were supposed to shut up and sit still. Don't start any new waves. Don't rock the boat. Do not disturb.

But that time is long gone.

Change is here, and it is accelerating. Sitting still is no longer good enough. Reinvention has become the basic literacy skill of the twenty-first century.

And you already are a reinventor.

All you need to do is to preserve this drive, this burning light inside that invites of all of us to make things better.

To try something new.

To go further.

To do more.

What an honor to share this journey with you. I can't wait to see all the amazing reinventions you bring into this world.

If You're Craving More, Here Are Additional Resources

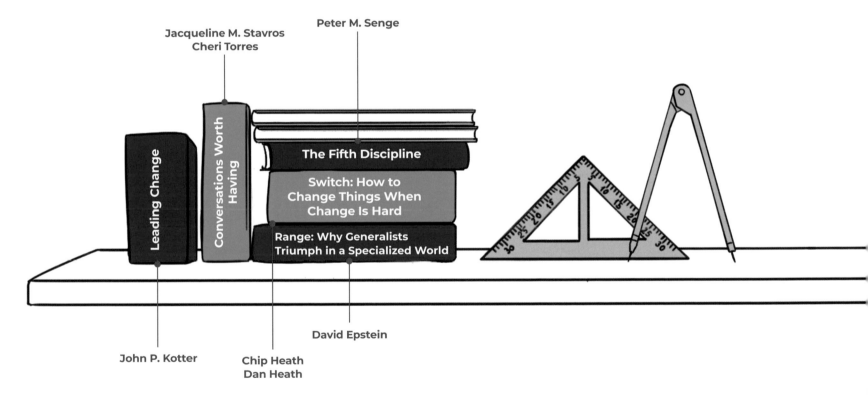

Jacqueline M. Stavros
Cheri Torres

Peter M. Senge

Leading Change

Conversations Worth Having

The Fifth Discipline

Switch: How to Change Things When Change Is Hard

Range: Why Generalists Triumph in a Specialized World

David Epstein

John P. Kotter

Chip Heath
Dan Heath

BOOKS

As we've done with Part 1 and Part 2, it's time to share outstanding books and resources for even more insights on how to reinvent yourself, your organization, or your community. We feature our topic here - and you can always get links to these resources and find even more helpful tools at **www.ChiefReinventionOfficer.com/resources**

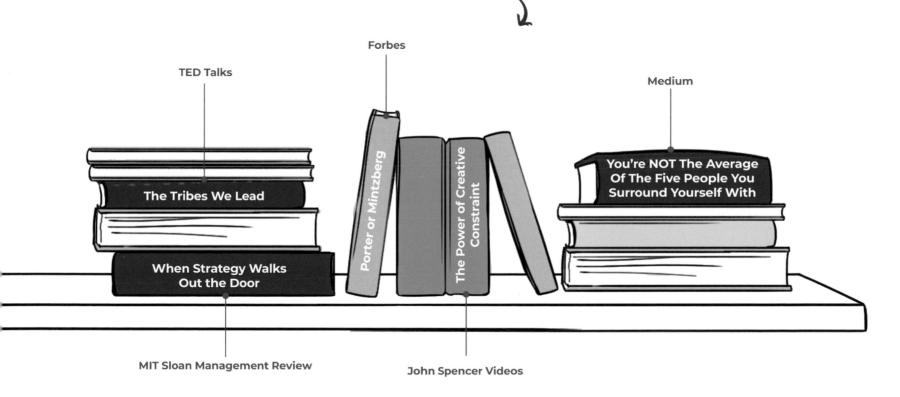

Forbes

TED Talks

Medium

The Tribes We Lead

Porter or Mintzberg

The Power of Creative Constraint

You're NOT The Average Of The Five People You Surround Yourself With

When Strategy Walks Out the Door

MIT Sloan Management Review

John Spencer Videos

ARTICLES

Notes

Change Is Not a Project: An Introduction

4   **On January 11, 2020:** Erin Schumaker, "Timeline: How coronavirus got started," *ABC News,* April 23, 2020, https://abcnews.go.com/Health/timeline-coronavirus-started/story?id=69435165.

4   **In the United States alone:** Anneken Tappe, "30 million Americans have filed initial unemployment claims since mid-March," *CNN,* April 23, 2020, https://www.cnn.com/2020/04/30/economy/unemployment-benefits-coronavirus/index.html.

5   **Andrey Khusid, Miro's CEO, explains:** I am grateful to Andrey Khusid and Sarah Beldo of Miro for the in-depth interview on the company's story.

5   **As the virus forced people to stay indoors:** In addition to an original interview graciously offered by Miro's team, I got information about the company's progress from Ron Miller, "Miro lands $50M Series B for digital whiteboard as demand surges," *TechCrunch,* April 23, 2020, https://techcrunch.com/2020/04/23/miro-lands-50m-series-b-for-digital-whiteboard-as-demand-surges/.

6   **In 2010, in the middle of another crisis:** Ranjay Gulati, Nitin Nohria, Franz Wohlgezogen, "Roaring Out of Recession," *Harvard Business Review,* March 2010 Issue, https://hbr.org/2010/03/roaring-out-of-recession.

6   **In 2019, Walter Frick shared a powerful:** Walter Frick, "How to Survive a Recession and Thrive Afterward," *Harvard Business Review,* May–June 2019 Issue, https://hbr.org/2019/05/how-to-survive-a-recession-and-thrive-afterward.

6   **From the Roman panic:** Bryan Taylor, "Tiberius Used Quantitative Easing To Solve The Financial Crisis Of 33 AD," *Business Insider,* October 26, 2013, https://www.businessinsider.com/qe-in-the-financial-crisis-of-33-ad-2013-10?r=US&IR=T&IR=T.

7   **It looked as if we had reached:** Francis Fukuyama, *The End of History and the Last Man* (Free Press, January 31, 1992).

7   **Although its foundations were laid earlier:** learn more about The Wharton School on the official website: https://www.wharton.upenn.edu/about-wharton/.

7   **As Steve Denning of Forbes puts it:** Steve Denning, "Peggy Noonan On Steve Jobs And Why Big Companies Die," *Forbes,* November 11, 2011, https://www.forbes.com/sites/stevedenning/2011/11/19/peggy-noonan-on-steve-jobs-and-why-big-companies-die/#23ea0272cc3a.

7   **Geoff Colvin of Fortune gives a similar number:** Geoff Colvin, "Why every aspect of your business is about to change," *Forbes,* October 22, 2015, https://fortune.com/2015/10/22/the-21st-century-corporation-new-business-models/.

8   **IMD-Lausanne's Professor Emeritus Jim Ellert shows that:** Jim Ellert, "Anticipating the Next Global Financial Crisis and Recession," *IEDC,* August 20, 2019, http://iedc.si/blog/single-blog-post/iedc-wisdoms/2019/08/20/anticipating-the-next-global-financial-crisis-and-recession.

8   **Beyond economic disruptions:** World Economic Forum, "The Global Risks Report 2019," 2019, http://www3.weforum.org/docs/WEF_Global_Risks_Report_2019.pdf.

8   **To borrow from:** I have referenced the beautiful quote in its original form William Gibson on page 25. You can learn more about William Gibson on this Wikipedia page: https://en.wikipedia.org/wiki/William_Gibson.

8   **That number is supported by:** Scott D. Anthony, S. Patrick Viguerie, Evan I. Schwartz, John Van Landeghem, "2018 Corporate Longevity Forecast: Creative Destruction is Accelerating," *Innosight,* February 2018, https://www.innosight.com/insight/creative-destruction/.

8   **One out of three public companies:** BCG, "How to Thrive in the 2020s," *BCG,* retrieved February 12, 2020, https://www.bcg.com/featured-insights/how-to/thrive-in-the-2020s.aspx.

9   **In 2019, to capture its journey:** learn more about Miro's brand on the official website: https://brand.miro.com/.

11   **By January 2015:** Nadya Zhexembayeva, "Built to Reinvent," *Chief Reinvention Officer,* initially published in the winter of 2015, downloadable at https://gallery.mailchimp.com/739aa10e270d2dde0df56f1d2/files/b23d4553-a6ba-4a8c-9b93-5db6edabda2b/.pdf?mc_cid=081fd13d86&mc_eid=3fbd0a11de.

11   **By April 2015:** Nadya Zhexembayeva, "To Hold On, Let Go," *TEDxNavesink,* April 28, 2015, https://www.youtube.com/watch?v=f4kySpcdvFg&mc_cid=081fd13d86&mc_eid=3fbd0a11de.

11   **In a world where you are expected to change:** Helen Barrett, "Plan for five careers in a lifetime," *Financial Times,* September 5, 2017, https://www.ft.com/content/0151d2fe-868a-11e7-8bb1-5ba57d47eff7.

22   **The first time I saw:** you can learn more about Professor Juan Serrano and his book on lessons of leadership from the Titanic disaster via his LinkedIn profile: https://www.linkedin.com/in/juan-serrano-transforma-47530814/?originalSubdomain=es.

22   **The idea of collaboratively writing a book:** learn more about Alexander Osterwalder and Yves Pigneur's books at https://www.amazon.com/l/B077MQ7W6D?_encoding=UTF8&redirectedFromKindleDbs=true&ref_=dp_byline_cont_book_1&rfkd=1&shoppingPortalEnabled=true, https://www.amazon.com/Yves-Pigneur/e/B00405XLBG/ref=dp_byline_cont_book_2.

22   **Professor Yuval Noah Harari made a strong case:** Yuval Noah Harari, "Yuval Noah Harari on what the year 2050 has in store for humankind," *Wired,* August 12, 2018, https://www.wired.co.uk/article/yuval-noah-harari-extract-21-lessons-for-the-21st-century.

22   **Professor John Kotter got us wondering:** John P. Kotter, "Management Is (Still) Not Leadership," *Harvard Business Review,* January 9, 2013, https://hbr.org/2013/01/management-is-still-not-leadership.

22   **Professor Everett Rogers' law of diffusion of innovation:** Everett Rogers, *Diffusion of Innovations* (New York: Free Press of Glencoe,1962).

23   **It is designed to serve you as a practical reference point:** learn more about the history of handbooks on the Wikipedia page: https://en.wikipedia.org/wiki/Handbook.

Part 1: Why Businesses Sink

32   **The largest man-made moving object at the time:** Oliver Smith, "Titanic: 40 fascinating facts about the ship," *The Telegraph,* April 11, 2017, https://www.telegraph.co.uk/travel/lists/titanic-fascinating-facts/.

34   **The last and most specific of the six:** You can find transcripts of the inquiries made after the disaster at https://www.titanicinquiry.org/USInq/AmInq08EvansCF01.php and learn more about John George "Jack" Phillips on the Wikipedia page: https://en.wikipedia.org/wiki/Jack_Phillips_(wireless_officer).

36   **The ship's mandatory sea trials began:** A wide range of references to the original materials on the Titanic disaster, including the sea trials, can be found on the Wikipedia page: https://en.wikipedia.org/wiki/RMS_Titanic. The sea trials are described in Spignesi, Stephen J. *he Complete* Titanic: *From the Ship's Earliest Blueprints to the Epic Film* (Birch Lane Press, 1998).

38   **First Officer William McMaster Murdoch was left in charge of the ship:** learn more about William McMaster Murdoch on the Wikipedia page: https://en.wikipedia.org/wiki/William_McMaster_Murdoch#Titanic.27s_sinking.

38   **In one instance:** Mark Garfien, "William McMaster Murdoch," *Encyclopedia Titanica,* retrieved July 20, 2020, https://www.encyclopedia-titanica.org/william-mcmaster-murdoch.html.

38   **However, as a slew of research:** William Craig, "The Limits To Learning From Experience," *Fast Company,* November 2, 2015, https://www.fastcompany.com/3052923/the-limits-to-learning-from-experience.

38   **Marshall Goldsmith and Mark Reiter in their bestseller:** Marshall Goldsmith, Mark Reiter, *What Got You Here Won't Get You There: How Successful People Become Even More Successful* (Hachette Books, 2007).

40 **The key was held by Second Officer David Blair:** Graham Tibbetts, "Key That Could Have Saved the Titanic," *The Telegraph,* August 29, 2007, https://www.telegraph.co.uk/news/uknews/1561604/Key-that-could-have-saved-the-Titanic.html.

42 **Lookout Fred Fleet, who survived:** Luke Salkeld, "Is this the man who sank the Titanic by walking off with vital locker key?," *Daily Mail,* August 29, 2007, https://www.dailymail.co.uk/news/article-478269/Is-man-sank-Titanic-walking-vital-locker-key.html.

45 **Let me add a few strokes to that picture:** This data came from "Welcome to the crisis era. Are you ready?" retrieved on July 26, 2020, via *PWC: CEO Pulse on Crisis,* https://www.pwc.com/gx/en/ceo-agenda/pulse/crisis.html.

45 **By the end of those three years:** This PWC report, "Navigating the rising tide of uncertainty," *PWC: 23rd Annual Global CEO Survey,* can be found at https://www.pwc.com/gx/en/ceo-agenda/ceosurvey/2020.html.

46 **Look up chaos across the wide range of scientific publications:** Jonathan Borwein, Michael Rose, "Explainer: what is Chaos Theory?", *The Conversation,* November 18, 2012, https://theconversation.com/explainer-what-is-chaos-theory-10620.

46 **You will also discover Margaret Wheatley:** Margaret J. Wheatley, *Leadership and the New Science: Discovering Order in a Chaotic World* (Berrett-Koehler Publishers, September 3, 2006).

49 **One statistic best illustrates the low survival rate:** Mark J. Perry, "Fortune 500 firms in 1955 vs. 2014; 88% are gone, and we're all better off because of that dynamic 'creative destruction,'" AEI, August 8, 2014, https://www.aei.org/carpe-diem/fortune-500-firms-in-1955-vs-2014-89-are-gone-and-were-all-better-off-because-of-that-dynamic-creative-destruction/.

49 **Kodak had been the staple:** Hiltzik, Michael, "Kodak's long fade to black." *Los Angeles Times,* December 4, 2011.

49 **Nokia had been the number one:** "Nokia owns 40% of global mobile phone market," *TechRadar,* January 25, 2008, https://www.techradar.com/news/phone-and-communications/mobile-phones/nokia-owns-40-of-global-mobile-phone-market-210162.

49 **Greg Sattel of Forbes explains:** Greg Sattel, "A Look Back At Why Blockbuster Really Failed And Why It Didn't Have To," *Forbes,* September 5, 2014, https://www.forbes.com/sites/gregsatell/2014/09/05/a-look-back-at-why-blockbuster-really-failed-and-why-it-didnt-have-to/#28656b751d64.

51 **As Steve Denning of Forbes puts it:** Steve Denning, "Peggy Noonan On Steve Jobs And Why Big Companies Die," *Forbes,* November 19, 2011, https://www.forbes.com/sites/stevedenning/2011/11/19/peggy-noonan-on-steve-jobs-and-why-big-companies-die/#2727a8fbcc3a.

51 **Denning's claims are supported by:** Richard Foster, Sarah Kaplan, *Creative Destruction: Why Companies That Are Built to Last Underperform the Market--And How to Successfully Transform Them* (Currency, April 3, 2001).

51 **There is more start up activity today than ever before:** Martin Zwilling, "A New Era For Entrepreneurs And Startups Has Begun," *Forbes,* December 25, 2013, https://www.forbes.com/sites/martinzwilling/2013/12/25/a-new-era-for-entrepreneurs-and-startups-has-begun/#3adff99c4bd1.

51 **Those startups also continue to die at a high rate:** Great survival data for one year and the ten year mark is published by the Small Business & Entrepreneurship Council, "Facts & Data on Small Business and Entrepreneurship," *Small Business & Entrepreneurship Council,* https://sbecouncil.org/about-us/facts-and-data/.

67 **For example, 1959 research showed that adding simple edge lines:** Paul J. Carlson, Eun Sug Park, Carl K. Andersen, "The Benefits of Pavement Markings: A Renewed Perspective Based on Recent and Ongoing Research," *Federal Highway Administration - US Department of Transportation,* August 1, 2008, https://safety.fhwa.dot.gov/roadway_dept/night_visib/pavement_visib/no090488/

67 **Since its inception in 1997:** I am deeply grateful to Dmitry Chernenko, Elena Chernenko, and the entire STiM team for in-depth interviews, excellent materials, and the willingness to test reinvention tools and resources to make them better. You can learn more about STiM on the official website: https://stimby.net/.

69   **With this commitment to reinvention:** Much of the information for this case came from the original interview with founder and CEO Dmitry Chernenko, but additional verification also came from academic research by Peter McKiernan, Danica Purg, *Hidden Champions in CEE and Turkey: Carving Out a Global Niche* (Springer Science & Business Media, 2013), 137-38.

69   **No wonder the company's driverless:** you can see the magic of driverless machinery via a video "Machines Spray Markings Onto Roads With Incredible Precision," *Tech Insider,* January 15, 2018, https://www.facebook.com/watch/?v=764506560423399.

Part 2: What to Do to Stay Afloat

80   **This desire to hold on, to cling to the past:** Scott Eidelman, Jennifer Pattershall, Christian S.Crandall, "Longer is better," *Journal of Experimental Social Psychology,* Volume 46, Issue 6, November 2010, Pages 993-998, https://www.sciencedirect.com/science/article/abs/pii/S0022103110001599.

80   **Dr. Heidi Grant Halvorson writes:** Heidi Grant Halvorson, "Explained: Why We Don't Like Change," *HuffPost,* January 5, 2012, https://www.huffpost.com/entry/why-we-dont-like-change_b_1072702.

81   **Neuroscience of leadership shows:** David Rock, Jeffrey Schwartz, "The Neuroscience of Leadership," *strategy+business,* May 30, 2006, https://www.strategy-business.com/article/06207?gko=6da0a.

81   **We also tend to see new things as a potential threat:** Diane Musho Hamilton, "Calming Your Brain During Conflict," *Harvard Business Review,* December 22, 2015, https://hbr.org/2015/12/calming-your-brain-during-conflict.

81   **2005 research, for example, suggested:** Elaine Rabelo Neiva, Maria Ros, Maria das Gracas Torres da Paz, "Attitudes towards organizational change: validation of a scale," *Psychology in Spain,* 2005, Vol. 9. No 1, 81-90, http://www.psychologyinspain.com/content/full/2005/full.asp?id=9010.

82   **Incidentally, did you know that every single day:** "How many oxygen molecules touch you in your lifetime?" You can find an answer to this and other questions on Physics Stack Exchange (a question and answer site for active researchers, academics and students of physics) at https://physics.stackexchange.com/questions/76838/how-many-oxygen-molecules-touch-you-in-your-lifetime.

83   **In 2018, out of more than 2,000 participants in our Global Reinvention Survey:** Nadya Zhexembayeva, "How often do we need to reinvent to survive?" *Chief Reinvention Officer,* October 1, 2018, https://chiefreinventionofficer.com/how-often-do-we-need-to-reinvent-to-survive/.

83   **The World Economic Forum's 2019 Global Risk Report mapped out:** World Economic Forum, "The Global Risks Report 2019," 2019, http://www3.weforum.org/docs/WEF_Global_Risks_Report_2019.pdf.

84   **The year 2020 is when the International Monetary Fund celebrated:** Hites Ahir, Nicholas Bloom, Davide Furceri, "60 Years of Uncertainty," *IMF Finance & Development,* March 2020, Vol. 57, No. 1, https://www.imf.org/external/pubs/ft/fandd/2020/03/imf-launches-world-uncertainty-index-wui-furceri.htm.

84   **Two decades ago:** Nitin Nohria, Michael Beer, "Cracking the Code of Change," *Harvard Business Review,* My-June 2000, https://hbr.org/2000/05/cracking-the-code-of-change.

84   **Today, according to global consulting firm BCG, we've gotten worse at it:** Boston Consulting Group put a great report for the start of the new decade, the 2020s, titled "Apply the Science of Organizational Change." I read it in January 2020 via https://www.bcg.com/featured-insights/winning-the-20s/science-of-change.aspx.

85   **It's a small wonder that companies seem to stay successful for shorter spans:** Scott D. Anthony, S. Patrick Viguerie, Evan I. Schwartz, John Van Landeghem, "2018 Corporate Longevity Forecast: Creative Destruction is Accelerating," Innosight, https://www.innosight.com/insight/creative-destruction/.

86   **Stéphane Garelli, a world authority on competitiveness:** Stéphane Garelli, "Why you will probably live longer than most big companies," *IMD Research & Knowledge,* December 2016, https://www.imd.org/research-knowledge/articles/why-you-will-probably-live-longer-than-most-big-companies/.

86   **By the early 2000s, the concept of VUCA:** Robert Johansen, *Get there early: sensing the future to compete in the present* (Berrett-Koehler Publishers, 2007), page 51, https://archive.org/details/getthereearlysen00joha/page/51.

87   **Singularity University co-founder Peter Diamandis and his co-authors of the 2020 book:** Peter H. Diamandis, Steven Kotler, *The Future is Faster Than You Think* (Simon & Schuster, 2020).

87   **Take Carol Dweck and her research on fixed versus growth mindset:** Carol Dweck, "Mindset - the new psychology of success," *Youtube,* October 20, 2013, https://www.youtube.com/watch?v=QGvR_0mNpWM.

89   **Consultants Paul Nunes and Tim Breene explain it perfectly:** Paul Nunes, Tim Breene, "Reinvent Your Business Before It's Too Late," *Harvard Business Review,* January–February 2011 Issue, https://hbr.org/2011/01/reinvent-your-business-before-its-too-late.

89   **The potential consequences are dire:** Matthew S. Olson, Derek van Bever, *Stall Points* (Yale University Press, August 25, 2009).

91   **As I show in my 2020 Harvard Business Review article:** Nadya Zhexembayeva, "Stop Calling It "Innovation," *Harvard Business Review,* February 19, 2020, https://hbr.org/2020/02/stop-calling-it-innovation.

91   **A team at the University of Toronto:** Jessica Galang, " University of Toronto study finds that Canadian attitudes towards innovation trail Americans," *Betakit,* February 16, 2016, https://betakit.com/university-of-toronto-study-finds-that-canadian-attitudes-towards-innovation-trail-americans/.

92   **As economic correspondent Alana Semuels shows:** Alana Semuels, "How to Stop Short-Term Thinking at America's Companies," *The Atlantic,* December 30, 2016, https://www.theatlantic.com/business/archive/2016/12/short-term-thinking/511874/.

92   **The average holding time for stocks:** Mark Warner, "Mark Warner says average holding time for stocks has fallen to four months," PolitiFact, June 19, 2016, https://www.politifact.com/factchecks/2016/jul/06/mark-warner/mark-warner-says-average-holding-time-stocks-has-f/.

92   **Almost 80 percent of chief financial officers:** John R. Graham, Campbell R. Harvey, Shiva Rajgopal, "The Economic Implications of Corporate Financial Reporting," January 11, 2005, https://faculty.fuqua.duke.edu/~charvey/Research/Working_Papers/W73_The_economic_implications.pdf.

99   **Brief and to the point, professional as ever:** I am incredibly thankful for years of learning from and supporting Hidria's efforts. I am particularly honored and appreciative of all the insights Dr. Iztok Seljak shared throughout the years, which contributed to the writing of this case. You can learn more about Hidria on the official website: https://www.hidria.com/int/sl/.

101   **In 2004, Hidria turned its business:** you can learn more about the company and find the source for data in my previous book, *Overfished Ocean Strategy: Powering Up Innovation for a Resource-Deprived World* (Berrett-Koehler Publishers, June 2, 2014).

102   **In 2011, together with:** learn more about SiEVA on the official website: http://www.sieva.si/en/about-sieva/introduction/.

102   **In 2012, the company initiated a new:** Feniks consortium is one of the key achievements that landed Hidria the title of the most Innovative Company of Europe: https://www.hidria.com/int/en/news/hidria-declared-the-most-innovative-company-in-europe/.

103   **In 2019, Hidria initiated the €8 billion:** Hidria, "The EDISON WINCI project as a transition to new technologies of electromobility," Hidria, November 2019, https://www.hidria.com/int/en/news/the-edison-winci-project-as-a-transition-to-new-technologies-of-electromobility/.

103   **Also in 2019, it united with eleven leading European institutions:** learn more about Project SOPHIA on the official website: https://project-sophia.eu/.

108   **That was the starting point:** learn more about Lush Fresh Handmade Cosmetics on the official website: https://www.lush.com/.

109 **...a Boston.com writer's take:** You can read more about the story in my article "Overfished Ocean Strategy: Five Principles That Make It Work," published by *Reflections* magazine in 2015 (Volume 14, Number 2).

111 **As of 2019, Lush has avoided producing:** the history of dry shampoo and its many benefits can be seen in Ceri Robers and Richard Skins, "The Naked Revolution," retrieved on July 20, 2020, https://uk.lush.com/article/naked-revolution.

111 **No wonder a 2018 Elle article:** George Driver, "8 Reasons Why Lush Shampoo Bars Are The Plastic-Free Beauty Product You Need To Buy ASAP," *ELLE,* June 13, 2018, https://www.elle.com/uk/beauty/hair/a21341509/lush-shampoo-bar/.

112 **Once a barely known company:** David Teather, "Lush couple with a shed load of ideas," *The Guardian,* April 13, 2007, https://www.theguardian.com/business/2007/apr/13/retail2.

115 **Where am I? At one of the many locations:** I am very grateful to Debbie Penzone, Charles Penzone, and Jessa Schroeder of the amazing Penzone team for the original interview and great materials for this case. You can learn more about Penzone Salons on the official website: https://www.penzonesalons.com/.

116 **Take, for example, RCA:** you can see the full Fortune 500 list for 1969 at https://archive.fortune.com/magazines/fortune/fortune500_archive/full/1969/.

116 **When General Electric acquired RCA:** Paul Richter, "General Electric Will Buy RCA for $6.28 Billion," Los Angeles Times, December 12, 1985.

116 **Pan Am had 150 jets flying to 86 countries:** Alastair Majury did an excellent summary of the company's story, "Why did Pan Am go bankrupt?," Medium, March 21, 2020, at https://medium.com/@majury1981/why-did-pan-am-go-bankrupt-aecc0d920575

118 **Then it added the Royal Rhino Club Barbershop & Lounge:** learn more about the Royal Rhino Club Barbershop & Lounge at https://www.royalrhinoclub.com/ and the details of LIT Life + Yoga studio at https://litlifeyoga.com/.

127 **The study asked 800 CEOs:** You can get a summary of the findings via The Conference Board News Release, which I retrieved on July 26, 2020, from https://www.conference-board.org/pdf_free/press/Press%20Release%20--%20C-Suite%20Challenge%202019.pdf.

127 **To answer this question, we will build on the research:** Mohanbir Sawhney, Robert C. Wolcott, Inigo Arroniz, "The 12 Different Ways for Companies to Innovate," *MITSloan Management Review,* April 1, 2006, https://sloanreview.mit.edu/article/the-different-ways-for-companies-to-innovate/.

127 **Their point is echoed in the dissertation:** Iztok Seljak, "Business model innovation as dynamic capabilities within a moderately dynamic industry," *IEDC,* March 2015, http://www.iedc.si/docs/default-source/Publications/doctoral-dissertation-iztok-seljak-abstract.pdf?sfvrsn=4.

127 **...we started with the MIT Article:** I learned about the work of Mohanbir Sawhney, Robert C. Wolcott, Inigo Arroniz from the MIT article cited earlier and am deeply grateful to the remarkable generosity of Mohanbir S Sawhney, McCormick Foundation Chair of Technology and Associate Dean, Digital Innovation of Kellogg School of Management, Northwestern University, for the permission to use and adapt the model developed by him and his team.

129 **After taking over the REI outdoor gear cooperative:** Aaron Hurst, "How REI's CEO's Quest For Purpose Inspired Him To Take Back Black Friday," *Fast Company,* November 23, 2016, https://www.fastcompany.com/3065943/how-reis-ceos-quest-for-purpose-inspired-him-to-take-back-black-friday.

129 **As a result, OptOutside was born:** learn more about OptOutside initiative on the official website: https://www.rei.com/opt-outside

129 **In 2013, the company reinvented:** "Adobe starts subscription for Photoshop and Dreamweaver," *BBC,* May 7, 2013, https://www.bbc.com/news/technology-22432171.

130 **That happened only in 1970:** Marnie Hunter, "Happy anniversary, wheeled luggage!" *CNN,* October 4, 2010, http://edition.cnn.com/2010/TRAVEL/10/04/wheeled.luggage.anniversary/index.html.

130 **There is an app for that:** learn more about the Carrr Matey app here: https://www.cartalk.com/content/carrr-matey.

132 **A 1-point improvement in CX Index score:** Rick Parrish, "Forrester's Top Customer Experience Research Findings Of 2018," *Forrester,* February 25, 2019, https://go.forrester.com/blogs/forresters-top-customer-experience-research-findings-of-2018/.

132 **Using LiquidSpace platform:** learn more about LiquidSpace on the official website: https://liquidspace.com/.

133 **Just the fact of collecting the data:** Adele Peters, "How Google saved over 6 million pounds of food waste in its cafés," *Fast Company,* April 24, 2019, https://www.fastcompany.com/90337779/how-google-saved-over-6-million-pounds-of-food-waste-in-its-cafes.

133 **Arizona State University took the challenge:** John O'Brien, "Innovative Cooperation at Scale," *Educause Review,* October 17, 2016, https://er.educause.edu/articles/2016/10/innovative-cooperation-at-scale-an-interview-with-michael-m-crow.

134 **Zipline, a San Francisco -based company:** you can learn more about the company and its business model at https://flyzipline.com/.

134 **With hundreds of machines already in operation:** Emily Canal, "The Hottest Food Startups in Chicago," Inc., May 22, 2019, https://www.inc.com/emily-canal/chicago-food-startups-inc-fast-growth-tour.html.

135 **Sawhney, Wolcott, and Arroniz offer a great inspiration:** Mohanbir Sawhney, Robert C. Wolcott, Inigo Arroniz, "The 12 Different Ways for Companies to Innovate," *MITSloan,* April 1, 2006, https://sloanreview.mit.edu/article/the-different-ways-for-companies-to-innovate/.

136 **Netflix, a company celebrated for its unique and powerful culture:** Patty McCord, "How Netflix Reinvented HR," *Harvard Business Review,* January-February 2014 issue.

138 **Maria Telkes invented the first:** learn more about Maria Telkes, her work and her life on this Encyclopedia Britannica page: https://www.britannica.com/biography/Maria-Telkes.

138 **Actress Hedy Lamarr helped:** David Brancaccio, Paulina Velasco, "The story of Hedy Lamarr, the Hollywood beauty whose invention helped enable Wi-Fi, GPS and Bluetooth," *Marketplace,* November 21, 2017, https://www.marketplace.org/2017/11/21/inventor-changed-our-world-and-also-happened-be-famous-hollywood-star/.

138 **Mary W. Jackson, the first African-American female engineer:** learn more about Mary W. Jackson and her work on this Wikipedia page: https://en.wikipedia.org/wiki/Mary_Jackson_(engineer).

138 **Melitta Bentz helped develop the modern coffee maker:** Chris Foulkes, "Melitta Bentz - The Woman That Invented Modern Filter Coffee," *Redber Coffee,* July 31, 2017, https://www.redber.co.uk/blogs/blog/melitta-bentz-the-woman-that-invented-modern-filter-coffee.

138 **Stephanie Kwolek invented bulletproof Kevlar fibers:** Kelsey D. Atherton, "Stephanie Kwolek, Kevlar Inventor, Dead At 90," *Popular Science,* June 20, 2014, https://www.popsci.com/article/science/stephanie-kwolek-kevlar-inventor-dead-90/.

139 **Praised for inventing the first telephone:** learn more about Alexander Graham Bell's life and work on this Biography page: https://www.biography.com/inventor/alexander-graham-bell.

139 **A chief innovation figure:** learn more about the List of female Nobel laureates on this Wikipedia page: https://en.wikipedia.org/wiki/List_of_female_Nobel_laureates.

139 **...the first person and only woman:** learn more about Marie Curie on this Wikipedia page: https://en.wikipedia.org/wiki/Nobel_Prize#Multiple_laureates

140 **The law of diffusion of innovations:** Everett Rogers, *Diffusion of Innovations* (New York: Free Press of Glencoe,1962).

144 **Kodak invented digital photography:** Michael Zhang, "The World's First Digital Camera by Kodak and Steve Sasson," *PetaPixel,* August 5, 2010, https://petapixel.com/2010/08/05/the-worlds-first-digital-camera-by-kodak-and-steve-sasson/.

144 **Nokia owned nearly 50% of the smartphone market:** Dave Lee, "Nokia: The rise and fall of a mobile giant," *BBC,* September 3, 2013, https://www.bbc.com/news/technology-23947212.

145 **Take, for example, the DriveNow car-sharing service:** learn more about the DriveNow Car Sharing and Car Club on the official website: https://www.drive-now.com/en.

146   **JustPark. a strategic investment by BMW i Ventures:** learn more about JustPark on the official website: https://www.justpark.com/about/.

146   **A fifty-year-old story of Rolls-Royce:** Rolls-Royce, "Rolls-Royce celebrates 50th anniversary of Power-by-the-Hour," *Rolls-Royce,* October 30, 2012, https://www.rolls-royce.com/media/press-releases-archive/yr-2012/121030-the-hour.aspx.

146   **Imagine you are an airline executive in charge of the fleet:** The Wharton School of the University of Pennsylvania, "'Power by the Hour': Can Paying Only for Performance Redefine How Products Are Sold and Serviced?" *Knowledge@Wharton,* February 21, 2007, https://knowledge.wharton.upenn.edu/article/power-by-the-hour-can-paying-only-for-performance-redefine-how-products-are-sold-and-serviced/.

Part 3: How to Make Your Company Watertight

155   **The term of unclear origins:** Climb Lean, "Jumping the curve," *Medium,* January 23, 2018, https://medium.com/@climb.lean/jumping-the-curve-3cf828d0154e.

156   **Start reinvention too late, and you are cooked:** Paul Nunes, Tim Breene, "Reinvent Your Business Before It's Too Late," *Harvard Business Review,* January–February 2011 Issue, https://hbr.org/2011/01/reinvent-your-business-before-its-too-late.

160   **Some engage the help of unique and previously ignored sources of information:** learn more about TrendWatching on the official website: https://trendwatching.com/.

161   **Let me illustrate it with a study:** Lester Coch, John R. P. French, "Overcoming Resistance to Change," *Social Science,* http://www.genesismex.org/ACTIDOCE/PDFS/ARTICULO%20COCH%20&%20FRENCH-Overcoming%20Resistance%20to%20Change.pdf.

161   **All workers are divided into four very similar groups:** Paul R. Lawrence, "How to Deal With Resistance to Change," *Harvard Business Review,* January 1969 Issue, https://hbr.org/1969/01/how-to-deal-with-resistance-to-change.

164   **In my recent Harvard Business Review article:** Nadya Zhexembayeva, "3 Things You're Getting Wrong About Organizational Change," *Harvard Business Review,* June 9, 2020, https://hbr.org/2020/06/3-things-youre-getting-wrong-about-organizational-change.

164   **Scientists from the Kellogg School of Management in the U.S.:** Elizabeth Wilson, Leigh Thompson, Brian Lucas, "Why Your Next Brainstorm Should Begin with an Embarrassing Story," *Kellogg Insight,* December 2, 2019, https://insight.kellogg.northwestern.edu/article/boost-creativity-brainstorm-embarrassment.

164   **At the end of a typical Kill Our Company day:** Lisa Bodell, "Want Your Business To Survive The Next Five Years? Kill Your Company Now," *Forbes,* August 31, 2018, https://www.forbes.com/sites/lisabodell/2018/08/31/kill-your-company-with-lisabodell/#3b73b75c6706.

178   **As I am writing these words:** Sapna Maheshwari and Vanessa Friedman, "Brooks Brothers, Founded in 1818, Files for Bankruptcy," *The New York Times,* July 8, 2020, https://www.nytimes.com/2020/07/08/business/brooks-brothers-chapter-11-bankruptcy.html.

178   **So did car rental giant:** Chris Isidore, "Hertz files for bankruptcy," *CNN.com,* May 24, 2020, https://www.cnn.com/2020/05/22/business/hertz-bankruptcy/index.html

178   **Cirque Du Soleil, the darling of:** Jordan Valinsky, "Cirque du Soleil files for bankruptcy protection and cuts 3,500 jobs," *CNN.com,* June 29, 2020, https://www.cnn.com/2020/06/29/business/cirque-du-soleil-bankruptcy/index.html

184   **Part of the Danish-based. family-owned:** I am incredibly grateful to Mateja Panjan and the team for sharing their story with our global reinvention community and providing detailed materials for this case. You can learn more about Danfoss on the official website: https://www.danfoss.com/en/ and get a sense of 24idea in this video: https://www.youtube.com/watch?v=W04KGx_hk-I.

190   **There are two people:** Karl Moore, "Porter or Mintzberg: Whose View of Strategy Is the Most Relevant Today?," *Forbes,* May 28, 2011, https://www.forbes.com/sites/karlmoore/2011/03/28/porter-or-mintzberg-whose-view-of-strategy-is-the-most-relevant-today/#684ed60558ba.

193   **The 2007 book by the brilliant thinker:** learn more about the Black swan theory on this Wikipedia page: https://en.wikipedia.org/wiki/Black_swan_theory or in the book: Nassim Nicholas Taleb, The Black Swan: Second Edition: The Impact of the Highly Improbable: With a new section: «On Robustness and Fragility» (Random House Trade Paperbacks, edition 2, May 11, 2010).

196   **Working with a range is backed by science:** Steve Martin, "When You Give Your Team a Goal, Make It a Range," *Harvard Business Review,* November 21, 2014, https://hbr.org/2014/11/when-you-give-your-team-a-goal-make-it-a-range.

197   **Many think that we constantly need to think outside the box:** John Spencer, "Think Inside the Box: The Power of Creative Constraint," *Youtube,* January 18, 2016, https://www.youtube.com/watch?v=IGyjGwSQXpg.

226   **Meet our team:** learn more about PRESIUM on the official website: https://presium.io/

Insert: Breaking Through with Business Model Reinvention Cards

237   **Pebble: Fund our smartwatch:** Verge Staff, "The Pebble smartwatch: a record-breaking Kickstarter success story," The Verge, April 11, 2012, https://www.theverge.com/2012/5/10/3011651/pebble-smartwatch-kickstarter-project.

237   **General Electric via its subsidiary FirstBuild:** Jonathan Shieber, "GE FirstBuild Launches Indiegogo Campaign For Next Generation Icemaker," *TechCrunch,* July 28, 2015, https://techcrunch.com/2015/07/28/ge-firstbuild-launches-indiegogo-campaign-for-next-generation-icemaker/?guccounter=1&guce_referrer=aHR0cHM6Ly93d3cuZ29vZ2xlLmNvbS8&guce_referrer_sig=AQAAAIhW9vAvh3gL-VHpfPZJv9nEABYrZRosx8RRQb_6mnuHI1UBWkYzrjAyopp-ZE8_fA2nTO0gvhKSvsxlt7JUwMRFz4-5sv30r2IbHyRnjnK5TkPBelzu9V93Y3dBhWiiqbL5qBe7h0sE5JzmgdgVJJS79jOc6H1ZfYEhmCsbl46t.

245   **We offer our Firefox browser to all users for free:** Vanessa Page, "How Mozilla Firefox And Google Chrome Make Money," *Investopedia,* updated on May 27, 2020, https://www.investopedia.com/articles/investing/041315/how-mozilla-firefox-and-google-chrome-make-money.asp.

247   **Dallas Theater Center:** learn more about Dallas Theater Center and Pay What You Can (PWYC) on the official website https://www.dallastheatercenter.org/pay-what-you-can/.

247   **Radiohead:** Get our In Rainbows album: Greg Kot, "Radiohead's pay-what-you-want download experiment pays off," *The Seattle Times,* October 22, 2008, https://www.seattletimes.com/news/radioheads-pay-what-you-want-download-experiment-pays-off/.

251   **Harley Davidson:** Kerry Ranson, "What does Harley-Davidson sell? It's not bikes." *Signature Worldwide,* November 4, 2013, https://blog.signatureworldwide.com/Training-that-Sticks/bid/323253/What-does-Harley-Davidson-sell-It-s-not-bikes.

251   **Verizon: Sells customer data:** Lily Hay Newman, "Carriers Swore They'd Stop Selling Location Data. Will They Ever?" Wired, January 9, 2019, https://www.wired.com/story/carriers-sell-location-data-third-parties-privacy/.

257   **Porsche: Choose your next ride:** learn more about Porsche Passport, now rebranded as Porsche Drive on the official website: https://www.porschepassport.com/.

259   **Richelieu Foods:** 700 or so employees manufacture: learn more about Richelieu Foods on the official website: http://richelieufoods.com/.

259   **Botanie Soap:** Gain a competitive advantage: Botanie Soap, "Brand Your Soap for More Sales," *Botanie Soap Blog,* June 24, 2020, https://botaniesoap.com/blog/brand-your-soap-for-more-sales/.

Index

Meet our team

Written by:

Nadya Zhexembayeva

In Ventures magazine calls her "The Reinvention Guru." TEDx Navasink calls her "The Queen of Reinvention." Dr. Nadya Zhexembayeva is a scientist, entrepreneur, and author specializing in resilience and reinvention.

As a consultant and an educator, Nadya helped such companies as Coca-Cola, IBM, Cisco, L'Oreal Group, Danone, Kohler, Erste Bank, Henkel, Knauf Insulation, and Vienna Insurance Group reinvent their products, leadership practices, and business models to meet new market demands and prepare for incoming disruptions. As a speaker, she delivered keynotes to more than 100,000 executives – including four TEDx talks. Nadya is the author of two books, including *Overfished Ocean Strategy: Powering Up Innovation for a Resource-Deprived World,* which was named Best Book of 2014 by Soundview Executive Book Summaries, and *Embedded Sustainability: The Next Big Competitive Advantage,* which was selected as one of the Best Sustainability Books of All Times by BookAuthority.

Designed by:

Maxim Gorbach

After graduating from one of the toughest tech schools of the world, Bauman University, Maxim reinvented himself as the co-owner and Chief Design Director at **PRESIUM**, a design and innovation agency.

Designed by:

Ilya Galushin

Trained in economics and investment management, Ilya is the co-owner and Chief Marketing Officer at **PRESIUM**, a design and innovation agency, where he also oversees new digital product development.

CHIEF REINVENTION OFFICER

Dealing with change is overwhelming. Just as we handle one disruption, another crisis looms on the horizon. How do you survive and even thrive?

Nadya and her global Chief Reinvention Officer tribe understand the struggle and help you deal with change by reinventing your products, processes, and leadership practices.

Our mission is simple: bring resilience and reinvention skills to 1 billion people — so that we can all ride the waves of change, rather than get crushed by them.

We are honored to have you on this journey.

PRÉSIUM

In our loud business world, separating a signal from noise is essential. From developing your strategy to communicating it with your stakeholders to training your employees on how to execute, PRESIUM is a one-stop-shop for your strategy, communication, and innovation needs.

We are a studio that creates visual communications to enhance your business efficiency. PRESIUM helps companies remain competitive by presenting their ideas in a brand new way.

CHIEF
REINVENTION
OFFICER.COM

BONUS

REINVENT YOUR BUSINESS MODEL

Breaking through
with Business Model Reinvention Cards

25
BUSINESS
MODELS

CASH MACHINE

A customer is required to make an up-front payment for all goods and services, even before a company covers its associated costs. The resulting liquidity can be used to pay off debts or to invest in other areas.

Examples

Groupon: Get a discount by paying for your product or service up front

Any B2B manufacturer: 20-50% deposit prior to starting the order

CROWDSOURCING
a.k.a. OPEN INNOVATION

A task or problem is solved by a group of anonymous users, usually via the Internet. Contributors receive a small reward or an opportunity to win a prize. Customers get engagement and positive experience. The company gets tons of ideas and solutions for free.

Examples

LEGO: Come up with a new LEGO set idea and soon you will see it in stores!

99 Designs: Send your logo design ideas that match the customer need — and if the customer picks you, you get a big chunk of money!

ADD-ON

The core product is offered at a competitive price, while the total value of products or services sold increases significantly due to numerous add-on options. The benefit to the client is the ability to build a custom solution that fits their specific needs. The key to you as a company is to offer high-margin add-on features and benefits.

Examples

Southwest Airlines: Anything including seat selection is extra

McDonald's: "Would you like fries with that?"

REWARDS-BASED
CROWDFUNDING

A product, project or startup is funded (usually via the Internet) by a group of investors who want to support the idea. When a critical mass is reached the idea is launched. The investors get an opportunity to pre-purchase the product at an attractive price. Other rewards can also be used. Newcomers use crowdfunding as an alternative financing process. Big companies utilize it for market research and product testing.

Examples

Pebble: Fund our smartwatch via Kickstarter in May 2012 and we will ship it to you in January or 2013

General Electric: via it's subsidiary FirstBuild, Support our campaign on Indiegogo in 2015 so that we can launch the Opal Nugget Ice Maker (and do some market research as we go).

E-COMMERCE

Traditional goods or services are offered through Internet channels, which reduces overhead costs associated with managing the infrastructure of brick-and-mortar branches. Customers benefit from convenient time-saving interactions and a wider range of products or services.

Examples

Zappos: Buy shoes (and much more) online and get amazing customer service

Dollar Shave Club: Get your razor cheaper than anywhere else — delivered to your door

CROSS-SELL

Cross-selling means selling additional goods and services to an existing customer. Here you are offering a replacement for what customer has already bought, a supplement or related product (typically at a cheaper price), or an addition that fits the customer's interests and needs. Usually companies easily provide products, especially in retail complementary, to need of cross-sell, while addition to no social customer as next on. This way made needs of po. existing company is mere with relatively minor changes to the existing infrastructure and assets.

Examples

BestBuy: Get a deal on a computer case, mouse and screen cleaning wipes when you purchase a new laptop.

Geico: Get a great rate on homeowners insurance

LONG TAIL

The main share of profits is generated not from large volumes of popular products but from selling low volume, or hard-to-find items. The long tail has its own niche market, it is beneficial where it can cover inventory and distribution costs, and is often a better indicator of a customer's need. A wide variety of products is offer & service the company, if you offer in sufficient quantities, the total profits from such small sales result in a significant final amount.

Examples

Amazon: Get anything and everything your heart desires

Netflix: Even the most boring documentary can find its audience.

Business modeling, fun included

Welcome to your newest reinvention tool: Business Model Reinvention Cards!

These cards help you structure, discuss, and develop projects. You can use them to clarify your thinking, engage your team in a high-quality discussion, or run workshops for your clients.

In the following pages, you will find 25 ready-to-use perforated cards — you can also cut them out if that works better.

Here are some general guidelines and options for the ways to use the cards, and you are welcome to come up with more. You can do this individually, in a small group, or in a large group divided into smaller ones.

1. Place the cards on a table. Go through each one of them to become familiar with all the different business model options.

2. Discuss the pros and cons of each business model with your team (or by yourself) by sorting the cards in the categories shown on the right side of the page.

3. You can always combine cards as some business models go particularly well together. During your brainstorming session, write down all the ideas of what the business model might look like for your company on sticky notes. Put all of them on a wall, a flip chart, or a table in front of you.

4. Refine and enhance the ideas you came up with.

5. If you are working in a large group divided into smaller teams, **present the best solutions** from each team to the whole group.

6. Plan the next steps for bringing new ideas into reality. Concrete decisions about who, what, and when should be done next as this is the best way to assure your efforts go beyond talk into action.

 You can use the cards to clarify your thinking, engage your team in a high-quality discussion, or run workshops for your clients.

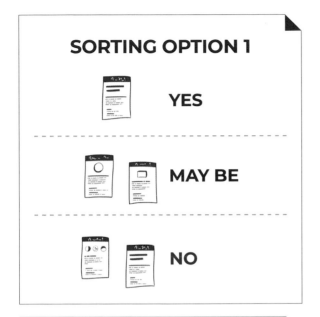

SORTING OPTION 1

YES

MAY BE

NO

SORTING OPTION 2

Organization preparedness

Industry impact

The core product is offered at a competitive price, while the total value of products or services sold increases significantly due to numerous add-on options. The benefit to the client is the ability to build a custom solution that fits specific needs. The key to you as a company is to offer high-margin add-on features and benefits.

A customer is required to make an upfront payment for all goods and services, even before a company covers its associated costs. The resulting liquidity can be used to pay off debts or to invest in other areas.

Examples

Southwest Airlines: Anything including seat selection is extra.

McDonald's: "Would you like fries with that?".

Examples

Groupon: Get a discount by paying for your product or service upfront.

Any B2B manufacturer: 20% to 50% deposit prior to starting the order.

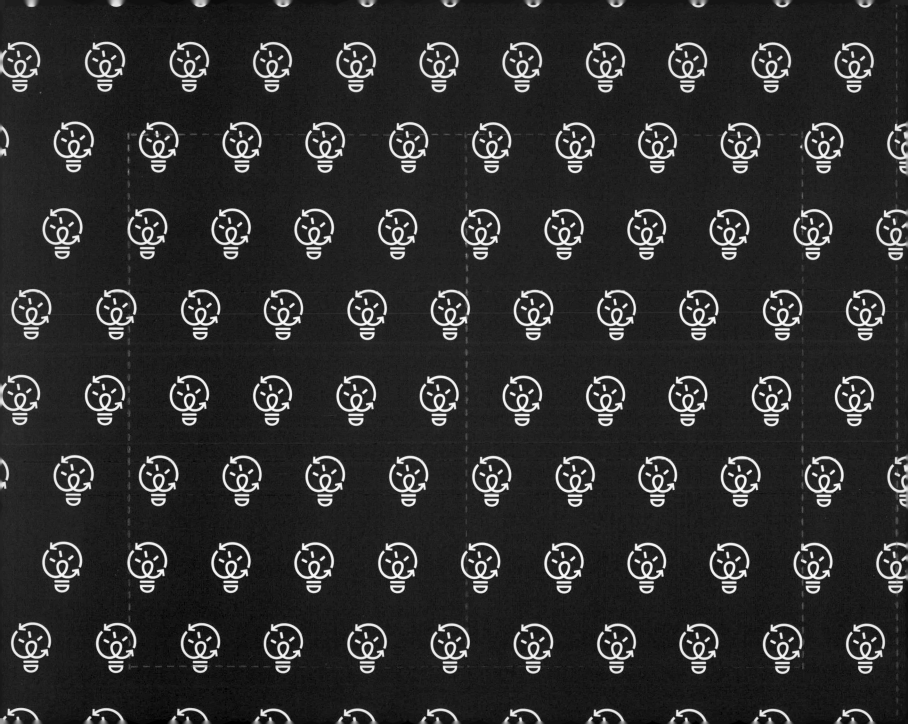

CROSS-SELL 03

Cross-selling means selling additional goods and services to an existing customer. Here, you are not offering a replacement for what the customer already bought, but rather a supplement or related product based on customer's interests and needs. Especially in retail, companies easily provide products and services that are complementary in nature. This way meets more needs of potential customers at once and generates additional income with relatively minor changes to the existing infrastructure and assets.

Examples

BestBuy: Get a deal on a computer case, mouse, and screen cleaning wipes when you purchase a new laptop.

Geico: Get a great rate on homeowners insurance.

REWARDS-BASED CROWDFUNDING 04

A product, project, or startup is funded (usually via the Internet) by a group of investors who want to support the idea. When a critical mass of funding is reached, the idea is implemented. The investors re-ceive a reward: Typically, supporters of the campaign get an opportunity to purchase the product in ad-vance at an attractive price. Other rewards can be used commensurate with the amount of money invested. Newcomers use crowdfunding as an alternative option for cheap financing. Big corporations utilize it for market research and product testing.

Examples

Pebble: Fund our smartwatch via Kickstarter in May 2012 and we will ship it to you in January of 2013.

General Electric via its subsidiary FirstBuild: Support our campaign on Indiegogo in 2015 so that we can launch the Opal Nugget Ice Maker (and do some market research as we go).

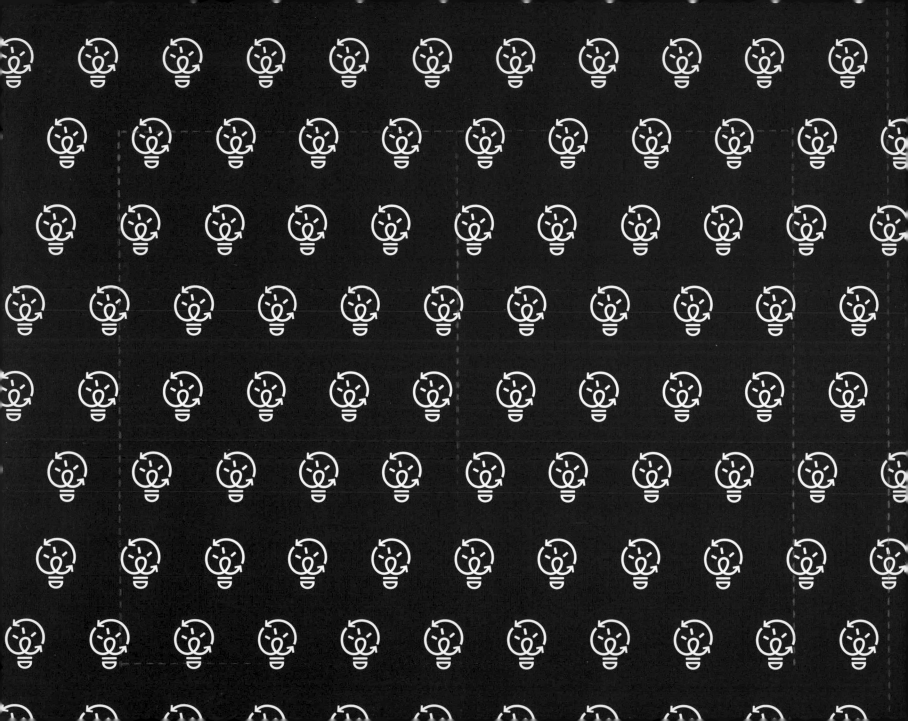

CROWDSOURCING a.k.a. OPEN INNOVATION

05

A group of anonymous users solves a task or a problem, usually via the Internet. Contributors receive a small reward or an opportunity to win a prize. Customers get engagement and positive experience. The company gets tons of ideas and solutions for free.

Examples

LEGO: Come up with a new LEGO set idea and soon you will see it in stores!

99 Designs: Send your logo design ideas that match the customer's need, and if the customer picks your idea, you will get a big chunk of money!

E-COMMERCE

06

Traditional goods or services are offered through Internet channels, which reduces overhead costs associated with managing the infrastructure of brick-and-mortar branches. Customers benefit from convenient time-saving interaction and a wider range of products or services.

Examples

Zappos: Buy shoes (and much more) online — and get amazing customer service.

Dollar Shave Club: Get your razor cheaper than anywhere else — delivered to your door.

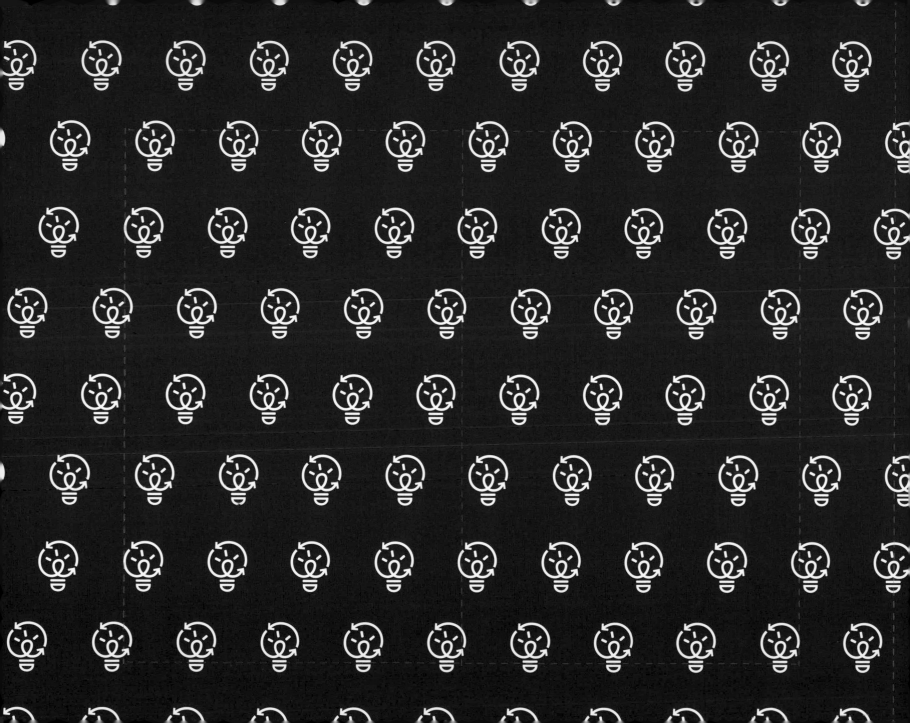

FREE PREMIUM

The company offers a basic version of the product or service for free and drives purchases of premium, enhanced product options. The free version is used primarily for generating leads to capture contacts of people and inviting them to upgrade to the paid version later on.

The franchiser, who owns the brand name, products, and corporate image, sells them under the license to independent franchisees, who assume all risks of local operations. The franchiser generates revenue as part of the income and orders of the franchisee and maintains considerable control over operations. Franchisees benefit from offering complete ready-made solutions under established brands and get detailed know-how and expert support.

Examples

SurveyMonkey: Get basics surveys done free with us, but if you want to ask your audience more than 10 questions, buy a premium plan.

Skype: Calls within our system are free, but you can always get a solution to call real phones or Skype for Business option for the entire company.

Examples

Subway: Own your own restaurant. We provide you with everything from precise recipes to shop layout.

Marriott: You get the building. We will give you all the rest.

To create value with this business model, you develop a solution, often based on a unique intellectual property, that can be sold under license to other companies. Your customers save money by using the product, service, or content that someone else developed while you benefit from a new source of revenue. Unlike the franchise, however, your customers have much greater freedom on how to use the solution. Often the solution your customers license from you is only a part of their business model, and they are free to license things from other providers or develop their own intellectual property (IP).

Examples

Google: Use our Google Maps software as a part of your business offer. (That's what Uber did, and see how much money it's making!)

Michael Jordan: Put my name on your shoes and pay me for it.

The core product is offered at a low-margin price or given for free, while the additional goods necessary to use the core product are sold at a high price, providing a significant share of income. Thus, customers are locked into a vendor's world of products and services, while the vendor is protected from losing its customers.

Examples

Gillette: Get our razor for peanuts. We make all money on the blades anyway.

Nestlé Nespresso: Yes, the coffee machine is shiny, but it only makes coffee with our pods.

The main share of profits is generated not from selling large volumes of popular products, but rather from selling low volumes of hard-to-find items. The long-tail business model benefits customers who have a particular niche taste or need. The company benefits when its variety of such products sells in sufficient quantities to add up to significant profits.

Examples

Amazon: Get anything and everything your heart desires.

Netflix: Even the most boring documentary can find its audience!

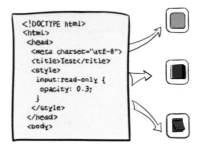

Often utilized by the IT industry, it is a development model that encourages collaboration and peer production. Products or solutions such as software source code, blueprints, and other documentation are made available to the public for free. Revenues are generated through services that are complementary to the product, such as consulting or technical support.

Examples

Red Hat: Get our software for free, and pay for technical support services.

Mozilla Corporation: Our Firefox browser is free to all users, but if you are Yahoo or Google, you pay us to be included as a built-in search option in the browser.

When using this model, customers pay only for what they consume. The actual use of a product or service is measured, and only then the customer is billed. Customers get greater flexibility, convenience, and better cash flow management, while the company gets better data for consumption patterns and is able to charge more per use.

Examples

Rolls-Royce: Don't buy our airplane engine; instead, pay us for the actual hours of the flight. If our engine is not performing, and you cannot fly, it's on us.

Car2Go: Who needs to buy a car if you can find it on the street, use it, drop it anywhere, and pay by the hour?

The buyer chooses the amount to pay for your product or service — or doesn't pay for it at all. Often, a minimum recommended amount is set as a starting point. The customer is allowed to influence the price, while the company benefits from growing a loyal customer base.

Examples

Dallas Theater Center: Get any seat in the house for as little as $1 per ticket.

Radiohead: Get our *In Rainbows* album with a "name your price" download.

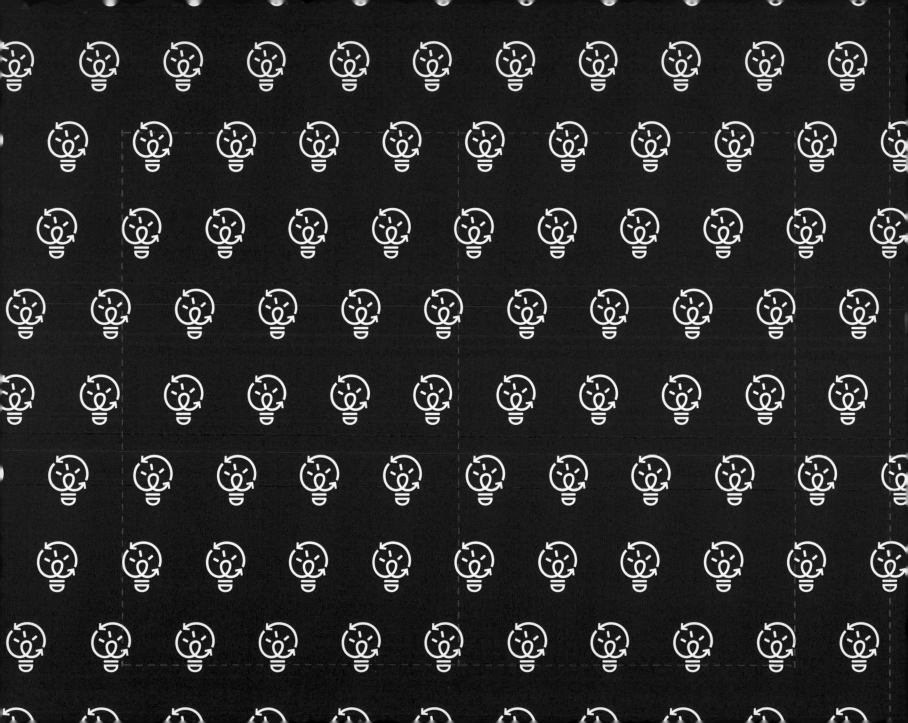

PEER-TO-PEER 15

Often referred to as P2P, this model is based on the idea of creating a platform where customers can meet and connect. Your job is to offer a platform (most often online) for users to interact, sell, and buy products or services. Users get access to one another. You as a middleman get commissions and fees for advertising on the platform.

Examples

Apple Store: Develop an app and we will sell it to all iPhone users for a fee.

Airbnb: A place where people who have a vacation home for rent can meet people who are looking for a house to stay at during their vacation.

AFFILIATION 16

Companies that use an affiliation business model sell some or most of their products and services through "affiliates," who are individuals or organizations that have a strong customer base and thus serve as a marketing channel. Affiliates get a sale fee or display fee while the company gains access to a diversified client base without additional marketing and sales initiatives.

Examples

Marie Forleo: Sell my amazing online course to your audience, and keep 50% of the revenues.

Kajabi: Refer people to our online business platform, and get a 30% lifetime commission from every customer your bring.

The product is no longer the most important part of the revenue stream — customer experience is. Instead of standing alone, a product is sold at a higher price point by pairing it with an amazing experience that makes people excited and motivated to buy. Customer experience is designed and carefully managed at all points of contact, long before the purchase is made, and long after the product or service is delivered.

The hidden revenue business model invites you to separate users from customers and asks that you think of users as part of the offer to your actual customers. Users don't pay for the service or product offered, but instead, access to users and data about the users provide value to customers. Users get free service, customers pay for a chance to advertise to the users or get crucial insights, and the company makes money in the process.

Examples

Harley Davidson: "What we sell isn't actually a bike. It's the ability for a mild-mannered accountant to dress in leather, ride through a small town, and have people be afraid of him." - Clyde Fessler, former Harley-Davidson VP.

CarMax: Car shopping made easy. There's no stressful-price negotiation, no aggressive sales tactics, only a hassle-free experience.

Examples

Verizon: Sells customer data to third parties. Buyers get insights from the usage statistics for their businesses.

LinkedIn: Even when you are using the platform for free, LinkedIn integrates targeted ads for services as well as jobs into your individual feed. By doing that, it is able to generate revenue from both free as well as premium users.

Product customization through mass production once seemed unreal. But today, mass customization uses modular products and production systems that facilitate effective individualization. As a result, the needs of an individual customer can be met in conditions of mass production and offered at competitive prices.

Examples

Dell: Design your custom-made computer online. Then all the parts get configured individually and shipped to your location.

Jimmy John's: Build a sandwich to your preferences using freshly baked bread and a wide range of ingredients in a matter of minutes.

Instead of buying a product, a customer rents it and pays for actual use only. The customer gets the value from the product without paying the full price while the company "sells" the same product multiple times. Both sides benefit from the efficient use and reduced downtime of the product.

Examples

The Home Depot: No need to purchase specialized equipment for your next home improvement project. You can rent it at Home Depot and pay only for the use duration.

Zipcar: Instead of buying or renting a car, sign up for a membership, and use it for a few hours any time you need it.

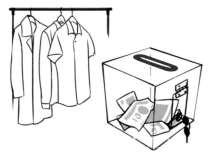

A product or service is offered to the "rich" audience at a premium price to support the needs of the "poor." The revenue comes from the more affluent part of the customer base. Although serving the "poor" audience doesn't make money, it provides economies of scale that other suppliers cannot achieve. An added bonus is a positive effect on the company's image.

Examples

TOMS Shoes: For every pair of shoes you buy, the company donates a pair to children in need in developing countries.

Bombas: For every Bombas clothing item you purchase, a specially designed clothing item of the same kind is donated to someone in need.

Value creation is partially transferred to customers in exchange for lower prices. Such a model is particularly suitable for those stages of the value creation process that have low perceived value, but actually have a high cost to the company. Customers benefit from efficiency and affordability while the company saves money.

Examples

IKEA: Customers are provided with the product location where they have to pick up the parts, then proceed to checkout, and finally assemble the furniture by themselves.

McFit: The equipment in the gym has written instructions. Members can create a personal training plan online. Coaches in the gym are present only to help with general questions and are not offering personal training.

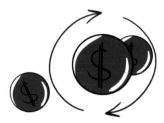

The customer makes a recurring payment, usually monthly or yearly, and in return can use the product or service. Customers benefit from the lower cost of use and guaranteed product availability, while the company gets a stable income stream.

Used products and materials are collected and sold or turned into new products. Raw material costs are kept to a minimum because materials provided by suppliers are procured for free or at low prices. In some instances, materials even generate revenue via a trash-removal fee. The company cuts costs while the customers get a planet-friendly product.

Examples

Spotify: Gain access to all songs on the streaming platform at any time with no limits, no advertisements, and enhanced sound quality for a monthly fee of $10.

Porsche: Choose your next ride with Porsche Passport. This all-inclusive, monthly vehicle subscription service delivers you a car to your door, includes unlimited car model exchanges, and covers the vehicles' wear and tear with insurance and maintenance trips.

Examples

Freitag: One-of-a-kind bags and accessories are made from recycled materials that had a different purpose in their previous existence.

Patagonia: Beautiful clothing is made from fishing nets, recycled plastic bottles, and much more.

A B2B model where the manufacturer invites other companies to sell its products under their brands, so it seems as if the products were made by these companies. Different sellers offer the same product or service under different brand names. Thus several consumer segments can be saturated with the same product at different price points.

Examples

Richelieu Foods: 700 or so employees manufacture hundreds of millions of pizzas per year. Finished products are furnished with the customer's branding.

Botanie Soap: "Gain a competitive advantage with our quality soap. Sell as your own brand".